To William "Bill" Colson, a dear friend, a motivator, whose motto was "You never go wrong doing the right thing."

And to all those who have affected the way I see and value people

A Candy a Day
Keeps the Doctor Away

Ewart F. Brown

Motivational Speaker
Building Positive Relationships

Copyright © 2018 Ewart F. Brown
All rights reserved
First Edition

PAGE PUBLISHING, INC.
New York, NY

First originally published by Page Publishing, Inc. 2018

ISBN 978-1-64214-780-3 (Paperback)
ISBN 978-1-64214-782-7 (Digital)

Printed in the United States of America

Table of Contents

When Two Lives Come Together 13
How Much We Care 15
Hands and Hearts 17
Building Premium Relationships 19
The Call—for Me or for Him? 21
The Dirt Ladder 23
Talk to Strangers 25
It Is Crazy 27
Talk to People 29
Friendship 31
Being Nice 33
Mass Ken and the Box 35
Human Connection 37
Living My Heart's Desires 39
Channeling Energies 41
An Angel from Montana 43
Smiles 45
Today Is the Day 47
The Lifters 49
Celebrating the Difference 52
Thank You 54
Monday Morning Adventures 56
The Speaking Mind 58
A Good Friday Story 60
Small World 62
Mother's Words 64
The Ripple Effect 66
Good Morning, Ewart 68
Connectivity 70
Making a Difference 72

Who Is Waiting?	74
The Life That Lifts	76
A Most Beautiful Thing	78
Life's Dry Powder	80
Ice Cream Cone	82
Every One an Angel	84
Turbulence	86
Here and Now	88
Memories	90
Shocking Shoppers	92
The Sweeper	94
The Empty Seat	96
Tell Me More	98
Dog Biscuits	100
Restoration	102
The Little Things	104
Lifesavers	106
What You Did Not Want	108
Just for Today	110
Turn Right and Go Straight	112
A Daily Prayer	114
What I Left Behind	116
Be My Friend	118
The Dancing Days	120
Being Nice to the Groom	122
Excited Thanks	124
No Stealing	126
Do I Have to Wait in Line?	128
Happiness	130
Mangoes Are Nice	132
Never Say Never	133
Start a Conversation	135
Stay on Top	136
Exceptional People	137
Just a Few Moments	138

Stay in Line 139
Planting Roses 140
Love Left on My Car 141
My Day 142
People and Projects 143
God's Time Clock 144
Thanks but No Thanks 145
Someone 146
Disappointment 147
Knowing Who I Am 148
The Second Angel 149
Glendora Barber 150
The Traffic Stop that Shocked 151
First Class 153
Living the Good Life 154
Munchies for Life 155
Rejected and Resurrected 156
From Me to You 157
Flowers and Dried Leaves 158
Burger King Worker 159
A Helping Hand 160
Fire and Grass 161
A Word a Day 162
A Line a Day 163
Sadness to Joys 164
Snack Packs 167

A Candy a Day is the verbalization of my
thoughts, aspirations, and experiences.

It is also a compilation of the thoughts of others.

These are the waves I ride on to get where I want to go.

They work for me and I cherish them, and
I am sharing them with you.

Let them take you places even beyond your sight.

God bless you.

Ewart F. Brown

A Candy a Day is not another shelf decoration, nor center table ornament, but a motivational piece to elevate our Care-Connections with people and Build Positive Relationships.

A motivational, inspirational work for people on the move with only a few minutes to catch a bite.

To sweeten our day, to nurture our appetite, to be eaten anytime, by anyone.

Please allow this material to help you live a more satisfied life and unfold some ingredients to make this world a better place.

Wishing you satisfaction, success, and joy on your journey, and it is my privilege to share in your journey.

Thanks for taking me along.

A Candy a Day is a collection of encouraging, directional, and motivational thoughts that can be used for daily living and one each day.

Most of these thoughts were generated by me when I found myself in life situations or in a meditative mood. A friend asked if I sat and just decided to write. No, that was not the case. These thoughts just floated in my consciousness, took a hold of me, touched me, related to my experience, and I was urged to write.

I had been writing and collecting them for several years and had no idea what I would do with them. But as I shared them with friends and noted that they were received with favor, I then decided that I would make them available to you as well.

At this very moment, you are reading this, because there is something here for you. This is my belief. So please allow whatever you find to make a difference in your life and in the lives of individuals you choose to connect with.

Apply your own personal focus and allow them to take you places. Wherever you end up, you would have experienced something, hopefully something nice.

I give God thanks for these thoughts, the collections, and my writings. I give Him thanks for what He will do for you. For it is amazing what God does with little thoughts and things.

Who Should Read This Book?

The one needing encouragement.
The one who desires to Build Positive Relations.
The one who wants some tips on how to get along.
The one who wants to make the community a better place.
The one who wants to make himself/herself a better person.
The one who desires to be liked by others.
Everyone should read this book.

WHEN TWO LIVES COME TOGETHER

Others may not remember exactly what you said or did, or even how you looked. But their brains will always remember how they felt in your presence.

—Arlene Taylor

My friend Flora, shared this with me: *"Your vibe affects your tribe."*

Thanks, Flora. This statement reminds me that who I am and the environment I create around me do affect those who find themselves in my space. This means my family at home, coworkers at work, partners on the playfield, friends at the party, worshippers at church, shoppers in the grocery line, traveler at the bus stop, the tired traveler at the rest stop, the little girl riding her tricycle on the side walk, or any human encounter.

We are placed here, wherever we find ourselves, to share ourselves with other residents within our space. Our very presence is a gift to the world. Some of us may have to intentionally do something to impact others. The rest of us may not have to do anything, just BE, like sitting with an attractive, warm smile or a pleasant face. It might be just how you said "Good morning" or "Thanks for the shopping cart" or "This is going to be a beautiful day."

Who we are or what we do will leave an impact on the observer. Who we are or what we do can affect how the observer feels at that moment and a long time after. As a teenager, Leo Scott, who was my godfather, did so much to make me feel significant.

He died several years ago, but even as I write, I am holding back my tears, because I remember how he made me feel as we worked together at his business. He made me feel like I was his son and that he was proud of me. He told and showed his business partners and guests that I was his son and that he was proud of me. I miss him so much, and I will be forever thankful for how he made me feel.

Daddy Scotty had no intentions to make me feel significant. He just loved me and said and did the right things.

In our encounter (Care-counter) with individuals, it will be our opportunity to care enough to make an impact and change someone's views of life.

When Shirley walks away from you, how is she feeling about that Care-counter with you?

How Much We Care

*People don't care how much you know until
they know how much you care.*

—*Anonymous*

When you walk up close to me, it will matter more how you make me feel than what you have to say, unless you have super pleasant thoughts for me.

Some of us gravitate toward individuals who are smart, or interesting, or who have the information we are looking for. But there are more people, I believe, who gravitate toward those people who have something to feed the soul. In other words, they have something that feeds the human longing of the heart.

As I have worked with thousands of people, in different parts of the world, I am continually impressed that what we humans long for most of all is a warm presence, recognition, appreciation, and caring feeling. We are sometimes comfortable with the food that feeds the head, but most times comforted by the food that feeds the heart.

People appreciate organization, good leadership, good humor, and reasonable social skills, but we talk more about how nice that person was. And often that meant how that person paid attention to people. "He/she made me feel good inside."

When I worked as a pastor, I was always reminded that my better sermons were not the ones with deep theological information, but those which told the people that I cared about them.

At those times, I saw the joys in the faces of the people. I felt the vibration of warmth with a desire to keep belonging to the family. I too was caught up in that warm feeling. I guess we were all affected.

Surely, several returned to the church because of the intellectual stimulations, for this is important. But more returned or chose to remain there, because they felt they were cared for.

I find it amusing that I become childlike excited whenever I have the opportunity to visit California. Why? Is it because of the temperature, the nice highways, the tropical-like vegetation? Not at all. I become excited because I would be spending time with family and friends. I knew that they cared for me and loved me. A similar excitement bubbles inside of me when I am planning a visit to Toronto, Jamaica, Philippines, or where there are friends and families. There, I would be safe and at home. I knew I would be loved and cared for.

People want to know and feel that someone cares. Please, when the opportunity presents itself, let us do all we can, whatever we can to make someone know we care.

Hands and Hearts

Everyone needs a hand to hold and a heart that understands.

It is thrilling to see two people in love walking and holding hands. There are other times when you see one person hanging on to the other. Then there is the child holding on to Mommy's or Daddy's hand. In 2015, my family visited Jamaica for a family reunion, and our granddaughter went with us. She was eleven years of age. I so much enjoyed having her on this trip and holding her hands while we went places. I am sure she felt safe in my hands especially since she was in a foreign country and did not know the people.

We all, sometime in life, need this safety, security feeling. We also need someone to run to for a favor, for assistance or advice, or maybe to take care of the dog when we are on vacation or to borrow an onion. We need someone we can go to who is like a good neighbor. We need one another, more than ever before.

But that is not all. There are the times when we need someone who will take the time to listen to our hurting, lonely, and broken hearts. There are so many broken and hurting hearts in our neighborhoods, churches, workplaces. And many of them do not have a release button, a button to touch and the pain goes away, no one to go to. So life goes on like an inflated balloon, ready to explode. Then after the explosion comes the fire that burns and hurts.

My walk in life finds me beside many counsellors who are there to help us with our problems and hurting hearts. But not all of us have money to pay for counselling, and there are some who do not trust counsellors. But we will tell our story to a willing, trusting heart that will listen and understand.

I must ask, can you be that willing, trusting heart? Yes, I know that most of us are willing to be good neighbors who will give someone a few eggs, tomatoes, or onions. While this is good, we are to remember, humanity has a hand (physical) and a heart (emotional). And both **hands and hearts** need our caring attention.

Can you imagine what it is like having hands but no feet, or vice versa? There are so many limitations in your life. Oh yes, I have seen individuals with no feet or no hands and who get along well. And I celebrate their experience. But I want you to see the experience of an individual with this limitation. Now please see someone who needs help with life's necessities, but has no one to help when his/her heart hurts and cries.

Maybe, you are that person who is a hand and or heart. You are able and willing to walk into someone's corner and give a hand or a heart. Then please know someone needs you. Or if you are the one longing for a hand and/or a heart, please do not give up. I am hoping and praying someone will come to you soon.

BUILDING PREMIUM RELATIONSHIPS

What you get from a relationship, usually, is what you had put into it. Try these and see what happens.

Determine what you can do to make this relationship work.
Demonstrate kindness and respect at all cost at all times.
Do not allow one's behavior to negatively affect yours.
Make the person feel significant.
Show interest in the person.
Expect nothing in return.
Keep building.
Be positive.
Be fun.

"Relationship" is the call bell that brings people together. It is the glue that keeps people together. It is the bulletin board that advertises what we are all about. More than ever before, I am hearing individuals at the workplace, at church, and at home expressing the importance of Relationships. I am hearing a line like this: "Relationship is everything." This means, whatever we do, if we want to be successful and positively effective, we must care about how our behaviors affect others, how we cause others to feel. Are people happy or hurting, successful or failing? Do those we associate with want to be around us?

Relationship is not born. It is cultivated. In some cases, a small Relationship seed has to be planted and carefully fertilized and nurtured.

Please remember, Relationship is everything. We either have it or we do not have it. But it can be obtained with work. And when it is obtained, our lives will become a vault of gold.

THE CALL—FOR ME OR FOR HIM?

Sometimes when we think we are badly off, there are others who are worse than we are.

It was one of those rare mornings. I was feeling emotionally low or blue, and I needed to hear a cheerful voice coming from somewhere. It did not matter where. So I did a mental walk-through of the individuals who could be available and able to brighten my morning. I finally settled on one name. He was usually cheerful and available at that time of the morning.

So I called him, for I knew he would cheer me. The good news was he answered my call and I told him why I called and why I chose him. He laughed and thanked me.

Then he took the reins of our journey. He talked on and on and on about the many things happening in the world. These events were indeed happening and should concern everyone, including me. But I was not ready to listen nor fix the troubles of the world. So I found this time with him very troublesome and annoying to me.

I wondered when he would finally run out of things to say, and I wished it would be soon. Finally, he was done. And I do not remember how it ended. Maybe, I was too tired and frustrated at this time.

What I do remember is at the end of our time on the phone, I realized that I was not feeling any better. In fact, I was feeling worse than when I placed the telephone call. And I remember thinking that maybe I should not have made that call.

Instead, I should have called someone else.

Sometime later that day, when my mind was settled, I reflected on what had happened with that telephone conversation. Then the realization hit me: ***The call I made was for him, not for me. He needed to talk, and I needed to listen.***

THE DIRT LADDER

That which they used in an attempt to bury your dreams are the same things that you may use to grow your future.

    This is a story I heard when I was a very young man. I always remembered it and applied it on my journey. The story is about a man who owned a horse. The time came when he wanted to do away with this horse, but did not have the courage to shoot it himself, nor have it shot. He pondered if there was a more humane way to put away this horse. He finally thought of a way to put away this horse. He knew this way would work for him and the horse. So he dug a deep hole and caused the horse to fall inside the hole. Then he began to shovel the dirt into the hole. The dirt fell on the back of the horse and then rolled off onto the bottom of the hole. The man was expecting to see the dirt rise higher and higher and gradually cover the horse.
    But the scene was different. For as the dirt rolled off the back of the horse and fell to the ground, the horse trampled the dirt and the dirt became a foundation, growing higher and higher, until the horse was able to step right out of the hole and was free again and lived. The story ended there. It did not tell us what happened to the freed horse and how it lived the rest of its life. And that is fine with me.
    But this story teaches me that the successful individual is the one who is able to let the dirt roll off to the ground and use it as a platform to step to higher and greater heights.
    My journey through life has not always been a bed of roses. The path had not always been easy and clear. And at those dark and murky moments, when I thought there was no way forward, I was

able to trample the dirt, use it as my foundation, and rise to greater heights, to where I am today. I am who I am today because of God, common sense, perseverance, my cousin, Sister Winnie, and Lynn, my wife.

Dirt is always being thrown toward us, or on our backs, intended to bury us. But like the horse in the story, we can rise above the grave and soar into the skies. Why not!

So now, I am inviting you to take the dirt which was intended for your downfall and use it for a ladder to success. Hoping to see you up here.

TALK TO STRANGERS

*When you talk to a stranger, you might be in for
the unexpected and that will be all right.*

Lynn and I were vacationing in Toronto, Ontario, Canada. We stayed at the home of one of my nieces. We had rented a car for the time we would be there. During the daytime, we went to places as vacationers do. But coming home in the evenings, I was always concerned about finding a parking place close. There were evenings when it seemed nothing would be open for parking. So I would drive around and around and wait for an opening. Someone, sometime, would have to be leaving. And this could be close or far away. Then there were a few spaces, a little closer. But when I parked there, I would have to have the car removed by 7:30 a.m., because that was a school zone. That meant no sleeping in for me. You are now feeling that parking was a challenge to our vacation. Minor, but still there.

One morning, about 7:20 a.m., I was walking to remove my car before it would be ticketed. I saw a gentleman sweeping the sidewalk by the school. You may say he was a **stranger**, since I had never met him before. I took the time to greet him and have a conversation with him. I commended him for the good job he was doing, keeping the area clean. He appreciated my observation. When he learned that I was going some distance away to remove my car, he kindly pointed to an empty lot, just a few feet away from where we were standing, owned by the school. He told me that I could park there. Wow! The empty lot he pointed to had only one car, and it was much closer than where my car was parked.

That was more than I could have dreamed of. I was very thankful to the gentleman and for the opportunity to park closer and not fight each evening to find a parking space.

But would this have happened had I not taken time to talk to the gentleman, a ***stranger***? Not at all. It pays to **talk to strangers**.

I am very aware that our world is filled with uncertainties and people with different value systems. And these drive us to be very careful, cautious, and suspicious about human contacts. This is good sense. But there are so many great people in our world and cities. We meet them in the stores, at the shopping mall, at the bank, at the post office, and everywhere.

And many of them have something good to offer, like a smile, a warm hello, or greetings and sometimes a story.

Standing in line at the pharmacy, I noticed another customer, a ***stranger***, who seemed a little restless. I reached out to him and engaged him in conversation. He painfully opened his heart and told me that his home was just burned to the ground, with his mother and himself only remaining. I was glad I gave this ***stranger*** the opportunity to release his pain.

He needed nothing from me but my ears and that I gladly gave him, and it cost me nothing and I gained so much by being there for him. Yes, ***strangers***, we were. But at that moment, it did not matter. It meant so much.

It Is Crazy

It is the broken twigs that the robin takes to make a bed for creating life.

In all of my life, at every intersection, I had desired that everything would be all right and the ride would be smooth. But that was surely not the case. There were several rough rides on the route. Those rough rides or circumstances, which were off my track and were challenging, surely were less appreciated and less desirable. So I wished they never were there for me.

I know you can identify with my situation, for you also have walked those rough paths or know someone who did. So let me tell you about a friend who walked this rough route, and I am naming her Jennifer.

I met Jennifer at my bank where she worked. We had several interactions, and I found her to be a delightful young lady, whom most customers enjoyed. Sadly, Jennifer accepted an assistant manager position in another bank, in another city. This was good for her, but not so good for us customers who appreciated her.

One Friday, at noon, I dropped in to see Jennifer at her new location. She was surprised to see me but delighted. She felt this visit was a divine appointment, since that Friday was a rough day for her and the last day working at that bank. She was unreasonably and inhumanely treated with very little or no respect whatsoever. She could not stand it anymore and had to resign. She said.

Then what would she do after? She had no idea, except she would submit applications. The next thing I heard was Jennifer was hired as an assistant manager at a bank here in my city. I personally welcomed her home and remarked to the staff that Jennifer was a top-quality personnel they were having. Then something else happened; in just a few months, Jennifer was offered the bank manager's position. She did not believe this was happening to her. Her words to me describing this were *"It is crazy."*

Yes, Jennifer was right, looking back at her journey. But look where she is now! As Jennifer and I looked back at her rough journey, she realized that it was there where she learned to work best with staff members and it was there she obtained the will and energy to push forward which placed her in a managerial position. Wow!

It was that bad situation which propelled her to become a bank manager. Henry Ford said it well in these words, "When everything seems to be going against you, remember that the airplane takes off against the wind, not with it."

So if you find yourself in a bad situation, remember, this might be the wind to take you to greater heights, or the door to the other *"crazy"* opportunity. Ask the robin what it thinks of the broken dried twigs. It would tell you that making a nest for her eggs and babies would be difficult without the broken dried twigs. My desire for you—wherever you are in life, be patient, be optimistic, be opportunistic, learn to ride on the wind, and walk through doors to opportunities. One day you might be saying, *"It is crazy."*

TALK TO PEOPLE

"There is no substitute for talking to people."

John (fictitious name) is a detective on the Cold Case Squad of Marion County, Oregon. He spoke to a group of Kiwanians one Tuesday afternoon. His presentation was captivating. One Kiwanian, at the end of the presentation, remarked that the presentation was the most exciting in recent times. I felt the same. What did John share with us which was so exciting?

He spoke of the many cold cases still remaining unsolved in Marion County and I imagine all over the world. But he told us about three cases which he and his team were able to solve. Yes, the cases were difficult with very little leads, but his team was able to solve them. And they were not solved by the use of DNA as is used in many present cases. But the cases were solved because he and his team took time to **talk to people**. In his conclusion, his punch line was *"There is no substitute for **talking to people**."*

Lynn and I were on a cruise where I presented one of my seminars. The boat was floating on the Mexican waters, so far away from my home. There in the cafeteria, while on the boat, I sat with my laptop, preparing for the next seminar presentation. I raised my head at the right moment to make eye contact with a gentleman. We both smiled and spoke to each other. He stopped at my table, and we both exchanged thoughts as if we knew each other for years. There were some things we had in common, such as; Michael, the name of my father and my son's middle name. He learned about me, and I learned about him. I gave him my business card, and he promised to connect with me. One never knows where contacts like this will end.

I can still see Michael's smile, and I am still enjoying his warmth. And even if I never meet him again, I am glad I met him.

On that same ship, we met a couple in the entertainment hall. We talked to them. On several occasions following that meeting, I met them and it was a warm feeling as we greeted each other.

We meet people every day. Some are familiar and others are not.

But I have a sure feeling that most people enjoy when **talked** to. The cold meeting is the exception and one that can be ignored.

Ladies and gentlemen, the world is a family. We need one another and are benefitted by one another. It is unfortunate that technology, though so necessary, has stolen us from one another. We watch TV, play games, or talk on the phone, while someone is longing for our attention. Someone wants to talk to us.

Talking to people helps in solving crimes. It also helps to Build Positive Relationships among individuals. It brings people together and invites even the stranger to smile at us. Please take the opportunity to ***talk to people***. The one you talk to may come around someday and talk to you or help you in the time of need. So as the opportunity comes your way, please ***talk to people***.

Friendship

Friendship is like a book.
It takes years to write,
but only a few seconds to burn.

All of humanity longs for **Friendship**.
We look for relationships which are close and cozy.
Some of us find it easy to develop such relationships
or **Friendships**.
Others struggle to find people who cherish
our companionship and presence.
And where no such **Friendship** is formed,
the search continues in desperation and emptiness.

Some of us know what it takes to form a **Friendship**;
one which is meaningful and satisfying;
one which makes us feel warm inside
and drives us forward to see the new day;
For in the new day, we expect to see and feel
a warm **Friendship**.
I know what this means.
I have felt it. And I still desire it.

However, this **Friendship** takes time to develop.
For we are careful about the arms in which
we trust our hearts and concerns.
But what is sad is;
After we have taken so much time to develop this **Friendship**,
something happens and suddenly it is gone.

All of our works and love slide down the gutter
and we are left with broken hearts and tears
and sometimes, some of us say;
"Never again".

How could something for which we worked so
hard and which meant so much to us,
suddenly be gone?
If you have experienced this lost **_Friendship_**,
please remember that there is One,
One who never stops loving you
One who never stops offering you His **_Friendship_**.
To me, He is the one and only, God.

"My God, I thank you for your forever **_Friendship_**."

Then there are the fortunate ones who are enjoying long **_Friendships_**

With a school-mate, work-mate, neighbor
With a spouse, or family member
or just someone dear.
Congratulations to you and hold on to that precious gift.
For **_Friendship_** is a gift, 365 days a year.

Let us exchange **_Friendships_**
It is the cuddle that puts us to sleep
The soft touch that wakens us in the morning
And the wind that keeps us cool during the day

BEING NICE

Show me the person who is happy, healthy and has many friends, and I will show you the person who is nice.

Lynn and I were on a flight from Detroit, Michigan. We were among the ones who boarded early, so I had the opportunity to observe others enter the airplane. One row in front of us, there sat a lady in the window seat who seemed to be alone. Then walked in a young man, maybe in his early forties. He stopped in the aisle and looked in the direction of the lady sitting by the window and said, "You are sitting in my seat. Get out." Hearing that, my heart burned. But I thought, maybe the lady was his mother or friend and that would soften the impact of his words. I paid attention to the next developments and noted that the lady immediately rose and relocated to the aisle seat. There was no interaction between them, so I concluded that they were strangers. Then I asked myself, "How could that young man speak to the lady with such disrespect?"

Could the young man have said, "Lady, my ticket says I am by the window. What does your ticket say? Is there a mix-up with our seats?"

Maybe that young man was having a bad day. He might have missed his earlier flight, which interrupted his plans. Or, maybe, that behavior represented his ongoing attitude to life and people.

But what of the lady? Maybe she was returning from burying her mother, sister, or dear friend, or settling a divorce dispute or any number of painful situations. Maybe she was hoping to have a seatmate who would be nice to her as she flew to Portland. Instead, her journey began with outright disrespect and lack of compassion.

My dear cousin Sister Winnie, who always encouraged me on my journey, was known to say, "Baby, be nice." I like this message. I am calling all of humanity to grab Sister Winnie's line. At the beginning of the day, starting at home, during the time at work or school, at the end of the day, even when we are tired and totally spent, let us remember, "Baby, be nice."

While driving home, I turned my car radio on and was searching for my favorite station. During the search, there was a conversation about the presidential election, and the language was not my type, but the commentator included a thought about **being nice**, which caught my attention. He said this: "Nice people are happier and perform better." I liked this. And I would like to share it with you. Could it be true that when we are nice, we feel better about ourselves and the world around us? Could it be true that when we are nice, certain chemicals are released within us that contribute to our energy, health, and attitude? Could it be true that when we are nice to others, we in turn receive niceness? All these are true.

Maybe, as we face today and each day, may we have the desire and passion to be nice. Nice to family and friends, nice to workmates and classmates, nice to neighbors and strangers. As the birds, flowers, calm wind, and pets are nice to us, maybe we too can be nice.

Maybe the greatest gift we can give to someone on any day is **being nice**.

Mass Ken and the Box

*The deeds we do are not measured by their sizes big or small,
but by how they affect others and how far in the future.*

High school for me meant living in Kingston, Jamaica, approximately sixty miles from home, which was a long distance.

I would be living with my eldest brother, who was renting a very small apartment, but enough for us two. All the things a sixteen-year-old young man needed were not available, such as food, laundry, and money. But my blessed mother, who had very little, did her best to provide me with what she could. The concern was how would she get these items to me sixty miles away?

Well, in those days, there were merchants travelling weekly from my town to Kingston to sell and buy merchandise. And they travelled by a truck, owned by a wealthy man in my town. So each week, this truck travelled to and from Kingston, with several merchants and two men who loaded and unloaded the goods. The two men were Mr. Cardo and Mr. Kenneth Williams. I want to tell you about Mr. Kenneth Williams who we called Mass Ken.

For the one year, while I attended high school in Kingston, every week, there was an interchange between Mass Ken and me. You see, my mother gave Mass Ken a **box** to give to me, containing my uniform, little goodies from mother to a faraway son. I emptied the box, reloaded it with my soiled uniform, and returned it to Mass Ken to be delivered to my mother. This was my life with Mass Ken for one school year.

What I want to tell you in this story is how Mass Ken was nice about this. Every meeting with him to receive or deliver the **box** was absolutely a matter of willingness, delight, and pleasure. Each time, I felt he wanted to do this for me. He never showed that he was tired nor that this was a bother nor inconvenience. He was always nice about this ***box***.

At that age of sixteen, I placed little value on what Mass Ken was doing. But now, as I reflect, I have great admiration for him. And I wonder, "How could he have been so nice?" I do not know, but I am forever grateful to him for his kindness. And each time I talk with him, I remind him of his kindness and give him thanks. That was all he knew, to be kind. Thanks, Mass Ken, from my whole heart for how you cared for my ***box***.

Mass Ken was nice and kind. He changed my life. I see people differently. My attitude toward helping people has climbed to a higher level. And I am comforted knowing that there are still nice, kind people in our world. I found this statement, "You seriously have no idea what people are dealing with in their personal life, so just be nice, it's that simple" (Facebook). One lady from Montgomery, Alabama, in a telephone conversation with me said this: "Let's make America nice again." Great! I fully agree with this. What about you?

Human Connection

*The mind often speaks to us and tells us to do something.
We may obey or disobey, attributing the direction to the human
feelings, only to realize that the voice we heard was that of God.
Let us listen carefully to the voices we hear, and as
we are prompted, let us act appropriately.*

In the middle of my busy schedule, I had a little nudge saying, "Call Lesmine." Lesmine is a friend of mine. We were both born in Jamaica, the same town, attended the same church and school. She now lives in Georgia. From our conversations, I knew that she had been dealing with health issues. So because of the little voice nudging me, I called her and she answered, and we talked about her health as much as she wanted to talk. Our conversation covered a multitude of subjects beyond health, such as Jamaica, since I had recently returned from vacationing there. It was a happy conversation. We ended our sharing time after about one hour talking. That very evening, I received this email from her:

> *Hi Ewart, Happy Tuesday evening. It was so nice of you to have called this morning. I was so sick with a frightening pain in my chest. I was in the process of taking one of my heart meds, which of course disappeared without reason.*
>
> *I was really at a low level. I thought that pain was going to take me out. However I found them. (Her pills) I truly believe God had you call me this morn-*

ing. I found out that while we kept talking about old friends, I started feeling revived.

I really needed a friend at the moment to bring me out of a place that did not feel good. I know God has a life boat for me all the time. I am not feeling the greatest right now but after this morning's experience, I am fine. (Smile) Thanks again my friend. May God bless you and yours.

It happened again just this week. I received a little nudging to call Yepsy, my goddaughter from Columbia. During our conversation, I shared with her a thought that Lynn had brought to my attention the night before. Yepsy was anxious to have it also because of a situation she was dealing with. Later in the conversation, I offered her some encouragement. That was exactly what she wanted to hear because of a situation she was dealing with. We celebrated together because of what had just happened. And all this happened because I listened to the little voice nudging me to call her.

I do believe that you also have heard a voice nudging you to do something, go somewhere, call someone. And when you acted according to the nudging, you saw why. Sometimes, we see why, and other times, we do not and may never know. I invite you to be in tune with the voices which connect with you.

So, the next time you are conscious of a voice urging you to do something, pay attention. You might be in for a surprise and a delight.

LIVING MY HEART'S DESIRES

Life is full of interceptions, but what really matters is where we began and finished.

What I am about to tell you is something which has happened to me repeatedly, which left me embarrassed and disappointed with myself. Has it ever happened to you? Maybe? Here it is.

Each morning before I face the day, or more often just when I drive out of my driveway, I pray this prayer.

Father, bless me today that I can bless someone for you. Give me life that I can help someone experience the good life. Connect with me that I can connect with someone for you.

And so I would drive down the highway, with my radio or CD playing, sharing the message for the day. I am still charged with good intentions. Everything is going to be all right today. But as the day and people come into my space, things change. And I forget my prayer and intentions. I would lose my cool just a little and may say a few things which I will later regret, saying to myself, *"I could have been more cool in that situation and maybe said nothing, or said it this way."* Then I walked away and would hang my head and cried in my heart. Why? Because I disappointed my God and the person or people in the encounter with me.

The point to note is when I left home, I had all good intentions. I wanted to be nice and to be a blessing and able to help someone experience the good life. Then what happened? Well, unfortunately, the human nature took over for maybe just a short time or I had just forgotten the purpose for which I was living that day and moment.

But when I look back, this is what I see, that people do not usually leave home determined to do evil or to be unkind. We really desire to be nice to all at all times. We know the purpose of life, and we want to make a positive difference in the lives of others. We want to be happy and make others happy, at work, church, or at home. But we are just humans on the journey of life, falling and rising and desiring a hand to lift us when we fall. That helping hand may be the hand of God or a friend or family.

I still love life and people and will continue the journey until the Lord takes it away. I invite you to come along with me. There, on this journey of life, are individuals waiting for us to connect with them and to give them a new look at life. We might be the only ones they will see. So let us not disappoint them. And even if we fall and fail, do not be brokenhearted, for that was included in the journey of life and growth. So let us collect the pieces and keep walking.

I hope to meet you on the journey, my friend.

CHANNELING ENERGIES

Spend little energy worrying about the difficulties ahead of you. Use your energy to develop strategies to overcome the difficulties, and take time to enjoy the muscles developed from exercising to overcome.

What I have learned is not to complain about the giants, but to rejoice about the fact that God is stronger than the giants.

I have also learned not to fuss about the dead end in which I find myself, but think of the opportunity and privilege of being in a new part of town and the new discoveries.

Do you see yourself in this scenario?

The telephone rings, and it is the secretary from your doctor's office. She asks you to come to the office to have a conversation with the doctor. Your heart immediately skips several beats, because you recently had a breast biopsy. In the office, the doctor explains that you had cancer, which needs surgery.

Now, your mind goes into overdrive. You are thinking of the surgery, pain, family, work, friends, hair, and the list continues. And this list can wear you down and leave you energy deficient. Right?

On the other hand, you could take this time to redirect your energies and thoughts to

- Recognize that God is bigger than your cancer and that He will be with you.
- Anticipate the opportunities you will have to be in the company of several medical professionals whom you have never met and maybe would never have met.

- Think of the messages of hope you will be able to share with neighbors, friends, and families.
- Once the word gets out about your medical condition, just imagine the dozens of prayers which will be ascending on your behalf from church groups and others.
- You may be linked with a number of support groups, and you will be able to add to someone's joy as others will seek to add to yours.
- You may even be wearing a new piece of hair, from the store or maybe your own.
- Then there is time off from work, home chores, and other activities. A change is always a good thing.
- The list of opportunities and advantages continue. I can only say you will have something to look forward to.

What I am trying to say is the next time you are faced with a challenge, face it with optimism and a positive attitude, because there might be something good there for you.

An Angel from Montana

When you place your day into God's care, you are to expect wonders. For God has a way of doing the extraordinary.

My friend Barbara Mattison posted her day's experience on Facebook. With her permission, I am sharing her experience with you in its entirety.

"I have to share a very special happening of my day today . . . Before I do that though, I am going to open my heart up for a glimpse into my very personal space which I so rarely do! I'm not one to post deep personal insight into my personal struggles let alone publicly on Facebook but I feel very impressed to share this . . . I will keep it simple and just say I have been struggling with trying to understand or come to grips with the cruelty in this world on many levels. I have felt the simple act of just being kind is diminishing . . . The depths of this struggle has been a burden on my heart for some time now.

"This morning I gave it up in prayer even before reading my morning devotional book. When I turned to today's date and began my devotional reading for the day it was focused on my exact struggles and how we cannot expect to be treated fairly in this life. That people will say and do hurtful things even when no one is deserving of that kind of treatment. My reading continued on to give promises of a kinder, loving, grace filled life in Eternity . . . I felt HIS peace and I gave a thankful prayer for meeting me right where I needed this morning!

"Now here is the rest of the story . . . I took my Great Aunt Ruth out to pick up her new glasses today and decided to take her to lunch on our way back home. We had a lovely lunch and visit. When it was time to pay the bill our waiter, with a big smile on his face said, "Your lunch has already been taken care of by a gentleman who just left." I was speechless and the waiter, noticing my shock, gave a little giggle and continued saying," The gentleman said to, 'have a blessed day from a silly old guy from Montana . . . !' Tears weld up in my eyes as I began explaining to Aunt Ruth what had just happened. She too got teary and people around us, who overheard the story were just smiling and wishing us a happy day as we left the restaurant. Random acts of kindness do still happen and I was blessed by one today by a total stranger!!! So many others were also blessed in their own way who witnessed this very special moment made possible by a 'silly old gentleman from Montana!'

"Well 'silly old guy from Montana,' you were my Angel today and helped heal my heart with your random act of gentle kindness!!!"

SMILES

Smile at a stranger, for that might be the only smile he gets that day.

Walking across the parking lot of our Safeway store, I saw a lady walking away from her car. Her eyes and mine connected. She immediately colored her eye contact with a warm smile, and together we warmly exchanged a hello. We both walked into the store, and after shopping for a few items, I found myself standing in the checkout line behind this same lady. I humored the checker to be nice to the lady, because she smiles at people. And of course, as you would expect, the checker threw a warm smile at us both.

This lady turned to me, who was standing right behind her, smiled again, and said, "I read it or heard it said somewhere, *'Smile at a stranger, for that might be the only smile he gets that day.'*"

I walked away from Safeway thinking of how many individuals living each day carrying heavy loads and are being burdened by life's activities and who are wishing that someone would take the time to give them a ***smile*** and change the temperature of their lives.

In my own life experiences, in almost all situations, whenever I give away a ***smile***, it always comes back to me. And when it does, it makes me feel good or better. And I wonder what it does for the other person to whom I gave it?

What do you suppose would happen if all of us, each day, walked around and gave away ***smiles***, whether we felt like smiling or not? By the way, here is a truism: When we do not feel like smiling and force a ***smile***, it usually affects how we are feeling. It makes us feel better. It may change our behaviors and those around us. It may produce positive behaviors.

So as we adventure and share space with people, let us *smile*. We have everything to gain from smiling. A *smile* says I respect you, I care, I am feeling fine, and I want to share it with you. A *smile* makes people comfortable with us and want to be in our company. A *smile* wins over a tough person and a tough situation. A *smile* increases our friendship population. A *smile* changes our attitude and increases our health. A *smile* tells something about us.

Since a *smile* does so much, isn't it good reason for us to be on the smiling wagon even more than we have previously been, especially since it is said that it takes fewer muscles to *smile* than it takes to frown? So dear reader and partner, let us *smile*. Let us give it away. It might be the best thing we can give away at any moment.

It was Mother Teresa who said, "Let us always meet each other with a smile, for the smile is the beginning of love."

For some of us, it will take practice and intentionality to *smile*. But it is worth it. So please remember, it takes just a little to *smile*, so the next time you have the opportunity, *smile*.

TODAY IS THE DAY

Today is a gift. Take it and wear it.

Several individuals have expressed their appreciation for me in the form of a gift. These gifts have come as sweaters, shirts, pens, socks, gift cards, and others. I have treasured these gifts and showed appreciation for them by wearing them.

I am realizing that each day is something new and that this new day is a gift. Yesterday was maybe a good day or not so good day. And there is tomorrow, but there is no certainty it will be here for you nor for me. All we are assured of is ***today***. So please let us be thankful for it.

As we have the opportunity, let us use ***today*** as if there will be no tomorrow. When you are nudged to make a telephone call to a friend or relative, do it ***today***. When you see a tired-looking person approaching you, give a warm smile, for you may not see that person tomorrow and ***today*** might be the day when it is really needed. When your family member seems lonely and buried in life's issues, take the time ***today*** to offer a hug of compassion and understanding.

Today comes with so much opportunities, including self-assessment, self-growth, caring for others, working on personal projects, etc. We will be better off when we apply ourselves to whatever faces us ***today***. Do ***today*** what comes to us ***today*** and not leave it for tomorrow. Tomorrow will take care of itself.

Today is your day. It will never come again. So be a blessing. Be a friend. Encourage someone. Take time to care. Let your words heal and not hurt.

You and I know of situations when someone said, "I wished I had done it yesterday," but never took the time to do it, so it never got done. Or another person said, "I will wait for tomorrow then I will do it," but tomorrow came with circumstances which made the task impossible, and it never got done. These scenarios float around us often and should remind us of the privilege of **today**. **Today** is the day to do it, and let tomorrow take a rest until it becomes **today**.

The Lifters

May the sun shine all day.
May the people around me be nice.
May everything be a Disneyland.

We do not like a sad life
We do not like a sad ending

We do not like injustice
We do not like suffering

In our childlike minds
We want the life that's pictured in the storybook
The life with a good journey and a happy ending

But that is not life
For life is a journey of ups and downs
The dirty and the tidy
And only in a few instances
Justice and rightness turn to triumph

When things go wrong
When we are treated unjustly or unfairly
The doors opened before us are usually
The doors of resentment, retaliation, anger, and gloom
And do we usually walk through?
Yes, yes, many of us do.
Rather than walking through those doors

We will do well to walk through the door called Discovery
For through this door is the opportunity
To discover
Advantages in disadvantages
Good in the not so good
I met a man the other day. He said
"I have something to tell you. I am a loader"
That is, here comes negativity
And he laughed at this
I did not laugh
For negativity is not my appetizer
Main meal nor dessert

I would have preferred a lifter
Someone to lift my spirits
Something to lift me higher

You too might have met a loader
They are everywhere
They are wired to load
All they talk about are the people and things
Which went wrong
But you know what!

We do not have to be like them
We can choose to be lifters
Being so busy lifting others
That we have no time to look down nor look back

Friend, we cannot change others
But we can influence how they think
By how we think, talk, and live
We can be positive and affirmative
We can be encouraging and uplifting
We can be lifters

Let us use our disadvantages as advantages
And therefore walk with confidence and purpose
This is the godly, successful walk
Designed for you and me

Celebrating the Difference

We do not have to think the same in order to live together happily. It is not only good, but healthy to be different.

    The call came home to say our cousin was just admitted in the hospital, having had a heart attack. This was touching to us and especially so since he was in British Columbia, Canada, only six hours away by car. From our troubled hearts, we prayed for him and wished wellness for him, but still wishing that we could be there at his bedside. That Saturday morning, I expressed to my wife that it would be nice to go and see our cousin after church. She said, "It would be nice." So, immediately, plans were put in place to drive six hours to British Columbia, and not long after, we were on our way. We called another family member to tell her that we were coming and not to disclose our plans to be there, for we wanted to have this a pleasant surprise. I like surprises.

    Once it was finalized that we were going to visit our cousin and that it would be a surprise, I began to look forward to the moment when we would walk through the door of the hospital room. I anticipated how our cousin would show his excitement. Actually, I was anxious to see this. And as we arrived at the hospital, entered the elevator, and walked toward the room, I became even more anxious and excited to see him and also to see the expression on his face once we entered the room.

    So now it is here, we walked into the room and our eyes connected. Can you see what is happening? Nothing. Nothing unusual. Nothing as I was expecting. The one thing that happened was my anticipation, my expectation was shot to the floor. You may say I was disappointed. All right, I will give it to you. You are right. I was disappointed.

But for a moment, look with me at my cousin. He is an easygoing guy, controlled person who expresses very little outward emotions. This is who is his. This is how he deals with life. And he is such a wonderful person. I love him just as he is. You might be asking if he ever said anything about our coming. Yes, he did. Later that day, he inquired about the trip. Yes, he did, and I am glad he did. He only did it at a different time than when I would and different from my expectation. But he did. And should it have mattered whether he said anything or not?

When I reflected on that moment in the hospital, I was reminded that my cousin and I are different and we express ourselves differently. And because we are different is no reason to be at odds with each other. I should not be disappointed nor upset. We can be different and still be happy with each other and with ourselves. And what is good for me is to learn to ***celebrate differences***. Be glad we are different and live. I also learned not to have expectations. Enjoy surprises.

THANK YOU

While the days are running by, so are the minutes. And unfortunately, so are opportunities. But why not stop for a while and take a little time to say "thank you"?

I will always remember the days of my youth. They were absolutely great days. I will remember what I had and what I did not have. But I will most warmly remember the individuals who loved me and did good things to me and for me.

I am writing this portion because I am remembering and thanking Roy Osborne. Roy and I lived in the same town in Jamaica. He was older than me and was already in the job market. He owned his car, which he drove to work daily. At this time in my life, I did not even own a bicycle and had no money for public transportation. I remember so well the many mornings I was on my way to school or just travelling to places hoping that a kind person would offer me a lift. But I never had to ask Mr. Roy Osborne for a lift. Whenever he saw me, he willingly stopped for me. He very faithfully did this over and over again. It is a delight to remember him and his kindness, even though it happened over fifty years ago.

One day, when I was absorbed in thoughts about people who had been good to me, I telephoned him and said, "Thanks for your kindness to me." Moments later, my friend Roy Miller called me just to have a friendly chat. In our conversation, I shared with him about the kindness of Roy Osborne. Miller and I agreed that kindness of the past is worth remembering in the present and future and should be communicated to the one or ones who had been good to us. So

Miller affirmed my idea of thanking Roy Osborne and then said, "We need to take time to say '*thank you.*'" Oh, he was so right.

In our busy lives, it is so easy to forget where we came from and those who helped us to get where we are. Therefore, I am pleading with you. Please let us remember those who have loved, been good to us, and impacted our lives. Let us remember to take time to say "*thank you*." We Americans go way out each year on the last Thursday of November to celebrate Thanksgiving. This is a great thing. But better still if we will expand Thanksgiving throughout the year, January to December. Remember those who have been good to us and tell them thanks. Recognize those who are doing good things for us and to us and tell them thanks. And remember, please, to include our families and workmates.

We know that people who are close to us are thrilled when we tell them that we love them or appreciate them. We also know that those who are close to us and even distant like it when we take time to tell them thanks. It feels good when someone says, *"I thank you."* It sounds good to hear someone say, *"I thank you."*

MONDAY MORNING ADVENTURES

Some see trouble, pain and fear. Others see sickness, poverty, and loneliness. I see adventures and opportunities.

Here I am. It is Monday morning, the beginning of the new day and new week. Lynn is far away, far, far away, like in the Philippines visiting families. And I am alone, and it is quiet, very quiet, not even the sound of a dog nor train. And since it is Monday, my mind is pressed with all the things and stuff to do. But suddenly, I feel the need to stop and realize that Monday morning is not only about doing tasks and filling my calendar. Rather, it can be and it is a Monday morning for adventures and opportunities.

When I think of adventures, I am thinking of doing something out of the ordinary—like stepping outside into the outdoors and watch a worm as it worms its way on the path to adventure or just getting its exercise and then wonder if it sees you sneaking onto its territory.

Like stepping outside the house and waiting for the first vocal piece of a bird and trying to figure out why it is singing and what might it be saying in its song. And could it be singing for you. And if it is, then say thanks.

Like listening to the bark of the neighbor's dog. Counting how many times it barks. Does it vary its level of barks and what could it be saying and why is it barking?

For some, adventure might be reading a book, talking with the fish in the tank, taking the child for a stroll, or going for a walk with your spouse or a friend. For another, adventure might be just doing nothing for a while. If none of these is in your dictionary of adventures, then find your own adventures.

When I think of opportunities, I am thinking of taking a moment, stopping everything, and listening to what life has to tell me. You see, often we are so busy planning for life and telling life what we are going to do. Surely, this has been good. But there is a time to stop planning and telling and just be still and listen.

Taking the opportunity to cause one to smile or laugh. This is good because we are told that laughter is like medicine.

Taking the opportunity to do something unusual—like, intentionally driving into the drive-through of McDonald's or Starbucks and pay for the purchase of the motorist behind you.

Taking the opportunity to e-mail, text, or telephone a friend or acquaintance who might need a little boost. All have opportunities. May we use them to make a difference.

I am encouraging you to adopt my **Monday morning adventures and opportunities** and make it yours. Allow it to work for you on Monday mornings and whatever times you choose, and you will notice a fresh air of excitement and personal fulfilment. And I suppose that this is what you want out of life, excitement and personal fulfilment. So, each day, please live for **adventures and opportunities**.

The Speaking Mind

*The mind often knows, feels, and sees, and will speak the task before us.
So obedience is the wise path to take when it speaks.*

Every one of us has had the experience of having the urge to do something. "My mind tells me that I should . . ." Some of us respond positively to the urge while others ignore it. Some of us who did obey the urge might remember what happened when we did what our minds told us to do. Maybe something significant happened or maybe nothing happened.

I will share with you just two examples of what happened when I obeyed what my mind told me to do.

My family and I were living in Massachusetts while I attended school in preparation for my ministerial career. One evening, I was very busy doing many things. I was busy, since I was a full-time student in the local college, doing courses by correspondence, taking a class in a neighboring college, being a student pastor, and caring for my two children when Lynn was working. But in such business, my mind asked me to take time to call and encourage a fellow student. I obeyed and called and encouraged Rocky. A few years later, I was on the seminary campus and was happy to meet Rocky, since I had not seen him for some time. He told me that he was attending seminary to become a minister because of that evening when I called to encourage him, because on that evening he was contemplating dropping out from college. Rocky is now an ordained minister. Did obeying my mind have something to do with Rocky's future?

Just a few days before writing this story, I took time to call George. We had a pleasant conversation and said goodbye. A few days later, his wife connected with me to say thanks for my call to George because it had come at precisely the right time. In a later conversation, she further explained why that call was very much appreciated. And I walked away from that conversation realizing that often when the mind speaks, we are wise to respond appropriately.

I am sure you too have had your mind speak to you, and yes, it will speak again. Please listen, apply your good judgment to have clarity about the direction you should take, and move forward. Remember, your future or another person's future might depend on your response to the voice in your mind.

A Good Friday Story

It takes little time and energy to connect with someone. So connect when you can because you never know where a connection will lead.

On a Good Friday, I was at the church working on the grounds. While working close to the road, I saw a truck driving by. I took a few seconds to look at the driver of the truck and waved at him. He waved back at me and smiled. I noted that he smiled. I continued working on the church grounds, pulling weeds. As I looked around, I saw a truck pulling into the church yard. I became curious, so I stopped to look a little closer, and as the truck came my direction, I noted that it was the same driver to whom I had waved a few minutes earlier.

We greeted "Happy Easter," and what followed is the reason for this story. The driver, who identified himself as Tim, said that he appreciated my wave when he drove by. He thought I was nice because I waved to him, and so he just wanted to stop by and talk about Jesus.

I was pleasantly shocked by this visit and the things Tim was saying. Though shocked, I enjoyed it very much and wondered how he could be so nice as to come to talk about Jesus. Tim did most of the talking, which was music to my ears.

He talked about his sinful past and how Jesus had loved him and saved him. He expressed his concerns for another family whom he thought needed Jesus. He said he wanted to pray for me. Oh, how sweet this sounded. For here I stood on the church grounds, supposedly a religious person, who should be advancing out to pray for others, instead, Tim came to me offering to pray for me. Wonderful and marvelous.

We had been together for about twenty minutes. Tim had remained in his truck. And when it was time to pray, Tim extended his hand from the truck, held mine, and prayed the most beautiful prayer. We said goodbye, and Tim left in his truck while we just kept waving at each other until he was out of sight.

I could not believe what had just happened. I still cannot. But this I know; it really felt good. God sent Tim to me that Good Friday morning. And Tim had a message which was refreshing. It was about how much Jesus loves us and wants to save us. Wow! Thank you, God, and thanks, Tim.

As a side note, I want to bring to your attention that all this happened because I took a few seconds to wave and smile at a passing truck driver.

Can you see and understand what a small, simple thing can do?

And so I reach out to God, asking, "Please direct me to what I can do to impact the world or even one person."

Small World

Be careful of the seeds you plant in the ground, for you may have to eat the produce whether you like it or not.

My laptop needed professional attention, so I called the computer shop to have it looked at. I spoke to the owner, whom I knew, and it was agreed that I would bring it to the shop. Entering through the door a gentleman greeted me. He was polite and very professional, but I was expecting to be greeted by the owner, to whom I had just spoken. And since I had told the owner what my concerns were about the laptop, I was hesitant to tell it all over again to this gentleman. Sometimes we want to tell the same story only once. So this gentleman and I agreed that I would wait on the owner, who was on the telephone. In addition, I was feeling less energetic and desiring to have a conversation with anyone.

While I waited in quietness, this gentleman said to me, "Can I ask you a question?"

"Yes, you may" was my answer.

"Are you a teacher? You sound like a teacher," he asked.

"No, I am not a teacher, but I am a preacher."

He gestured me by saying both are similar. We laughed. He wanted to know where I had preached, and I gave him a list of places my family and I have been. He seemed curious and cautiously asked if I belonged to any particular denomination. "Yes, I am a Seventh-day Adventist." He smiled and responded, "I am also one." This gave me a sudden burst of energy, and I wanted to know where he worshipped. Yes, he worshipped in the same city where I had pastored last, before my retirement. We knew the same people, and our conversation was now sailing on smoother waters. We were connected. We had things in common.

This, our world, is a ***small world***. We never know whom we will encounter and under what circumstances. Therefore, it makes great sense to be civil to all those we meet. There are so many reasons why it pays to be good to everyone. Just to cite a few reasons:

You might belong to the same church family.

You might be related by blood or marriage.

This might be your opportunity to create an impact.

You might meet again when you have some needs.

There is joy and peace in pleasant encounters.

Since my first meeting with this gentleman, I have had reason to return to the shop several times, and each time, I had the delight to converse with this gentleman. It was like meeting an old friend again. At our last meeting, he requested my contact information, which I provided with pleasure. He was a delightful person.

The next time we meet a stranger, please let us be nice. For this is a ***small world***. We never know where we both come from nor where we will meet again, nor under what circumstances.

Mother's Words

*Mother's words might be good for you, but only if you
live them and more true if they are timeless.*

Jamaica, West Indies, was the place of my birth several years ago. As a part of the culture then, it was taught and expected that individuals would greet one another whenever they met. It was more true for us children to initiate the greetings when we met adults and would say, "Good morning, Maas Sammy" or whatever the greeting would be. If we failed to do this, we could be reported to our parents or scolded on the spot.

This is a sad observation. Since I came to North America, greetings among people are less important. More people tend to look straight ahead, turn their heads away, or look toward the ground, rather than look at you and extend a greeting. But not on this sunny Tuesday morning, which I will always remember and I am about to tell you.

I was walking toward the medical building, and approaching me was a couple. I recognized they were born in another country, and I predicted that this was going to be a cold meeting between us. But before I greeted them, the gentleman looked straight at me and said, "Hi, good morning." Oh yes, I responded with a "Good morning" and a smile and was shocked for I did not expect this behavior. We walked past one another, but I was compelled to visit this couple, so I stopped in my tracks, turned, and walked toward them and got their attention.

I told the couple how I appreciated them greeting me for many others would have walked past without saying a word to me. The gentleman piped up. "When I was a child in Mexico, my mother taught me that whenever I met someone, to say, 'Hi, hello.' So that's why." Then I thought, "Good for you, mother in Mexico."

Dear reader, whether you are a mother in Mexico, parent, guardian, or just a good citizen, extending a warm greeting to the person you meet is always a good thing. It did good for this couple and me, for it broke the silence, removed barriers, opened doors, and provided opportunity for building friendship. The next time I meet this couple, our greeting will have so much meaning and warmth. And if I do not meet them, I hope they will continue to do **mother's words**. Say, "Hi, hello."

The next time someone is approaching you, will you take the risk and time to break the silence by extending a greeting? Then watch the response you will receive. If one person was cold and indifferent, please do not give up. Your warmth is coming; the next person might be the one to cheer you and who needed it most.

Break the silence, build opportunities with **mother's words**. "Hi, hello."

The Ripple Effect

The vegetable you grow in one location often finds itself travelling to other locations, and people from all over the country enjoy your produce. So keep on planting your vegetables, for you never know who will eat your produce.

Have you ever walked into an establishment and were greeted by an employee who was cheerful or grouchy? Oh yes, you have, for this happens often. In fact, whenever I encounter a cheerful employee, I remember to take the time to affirm this cheerful behavior. And whenever I encounter a grouchy employee, I attempt to create an environment that might change grouchiness to cheerfulness, and often this works.

What makes grouchy employees? There is a multitude of factors. And this writing will not address this. On the other hand, what makes cheerful employees? Again, there is a multitude of factors. But in this section, I will draw your attention to just one event.

I walked into the floral department of a Safeway store, where I had been several times previously. On this particular day, more than any previous day, the guardian of that department was exceptionally resplendent and as bright as the brightest flowers surrounding her. She was covered and colored with smiles and pleasantness. And I was compelled to inquire about the reason for her extra measure of flower qualities. I was interested to hear her story and even expected to hear that she just fell in love, got engaged, or won the lottery. But no, it was none of the above.

She told me the story. A customer living in California called her store and requested that she make a colorful bouquet, to be picked up by someone here in Oregon. So she went on to make this colorful bouquet to meet the expectation of the California customer. When her work was completed, she took a picture and forwarded it on to the California customer. The picture represented all the customer wanted, who expressed total satisfaction. It was everything she wanted.

Wow! My Safeway employee friend was so satisfied and pleased that she did such a great job. She was pleased that a customer so far away, in California, filled her cup with appreciation. I wished the California satisfied customer could have seen what her affirmation did to a floral employee hundreds of miles away.

Observing the excitement of this Safeway satisfied employee, I too began to experience some excitement and joy. You see, excitement and joy tend to travel from people to people and place to place. It has a *ripple* effect. It will go on and on and on.

Our affirmations will go ahead of us, and one never knows how many individuals they will touch. May we, at every opportunity, lift someone by offering positivity, cheerfulness, and affirmation. We never know where they will travel.

Good Morning, Ewart

It takes only a few minutes to make one's day.

Really, I was not having a bad day. Things were going well for me. But suddenly things changed for the better, because of an e-mail I received from Bruce. It said, very simply but profoundly, *"Good morning, Ewart. I hope you have a great day."*

Wow! And I stopped all I was doing, and for minutes I remained still, digesting and enjoying these few words. You see, I was not expecting these words from Bruce. We do business together and are in meetings together and would have expected a business correspondence from him. You mean, Bruce was thinking of me, Ewart, and how I was doing? This blew my mind. This is amazing. This is wonderful, transforming, and motivational. For soon after this, I thought of a few individuals who would not be expecting to hear from me. So immediately I sent e-mail messages to them, just like the one I received from Bruce. Thanks, Bruce. You made my day, and through me, you will be touching others whom you do not even know and may never know. Just think of how many hearts might be made cheerful because of you! And what is amazing is it took you only a few minutes to e-mail me.

Just a short time after I received this "cheer up" e-mail from Bruce, I was relaxing, going over a few things, when suddenly my cell phone alerted me that a message was left for me.

It was Cindy. Here is her message: *"Good morning! You are in my thoughts this morning and I hope you are having a lovely day."*

Oh, dear reader, this makes a difference in my life, and I am sure it would do marvelous for many others, maybe you also.

As you know very well, there are times during the year when mails, e-mails, telephone calls, etc., are busy making connections between people. Such times as Christmas, Easter, birthdays, anniversaries, etc. This is great. Let us continue doing this. Let us also remember that between these special days, so much may be happening to our contacts. There might be issues going on, dealing with loneliness, finances, health, work, family, and the list extends. At these times, we appreciate knowing that someone cares and is thinking of us.

So, I am putting a buzz in your ears. I am encouraging you to send a message to those you know best and love most, and remember also those whom you know less and love less. For everyone can use a little package of encouragement. Sometimes all we want to know is someone is thinking of us. Why not send a message now? It will take only a few minutes.

Connectivity

More than all the wealth in the world that you can offer me, what I desire most is just a piece of you.

When my life is just life, please say to me
  "I appreciate you"
  "I value you"
  "I care"
  "I love you"
  "Things will be different between us from now on"

When my life is a challenge and I am filled with
Doubt, self-hatred, anxiety, discouragement
Failure and loneliness

Please let me see in your eyes and hear in your voice
Something that tells me that
You understand
You care
We are connected
And everything is going to be all right

There are many things you and I long for and strive for, such as education, money, vacation, nice home, nice car, etc., but nothing seems to replace the longing for **connectivity** with someone whom we care about.

In some cases, when this **connectivity** is present, not many other things really matter.

It was shocking to me when I realized the importance of human ***connectivity***. You see, I had been pastoring for several years and felt very successful in everything I did. But when Gary Parks and I pastored together and we talked about relationships, it came to my attention that with all I was and did, I did not have any real connections with anyone outside my family. I mean, heart-to-heart connections. And this was what I wanted. And realizing this, I cried miserably.

This is what Larry Crabb wrote about ***connectivity***: "Connecting . . . is what we most want, what we most lack, what we most fear will never be ours . . . The deepest urge in every human heart is to be in relationship with someone who absolutely delights in us" (Larry Crabb, *Connecting*, 45).

How do you feel about your connections? Are you comfortably connected with anyone, someone with whom you can leave your heart and know it will be safe? I honestly hope you have someone. And if you do not, I hope you will find someone.

The heart has two functions, nourishing and cleansing, and together they work for the betterment of the whole body. Two of us, two hearts, connected and working together, may make life a better experience. ***Connectivity*** is life at its utmost.

MAKING A DIFFERENCE

*Some go for a walk and run into a fortune.
Others go on a mission and accomplish their goal.*

Please allow me to suggest that each new day that comes to us brings privileges and opportunities. As you read this portion, it should remind you that you are being given the gift of life and comprehension. And you are to be thankful for this.

But along with the privileges we have, there are still more privileges and opportunities. They are ours to be used to **make a difference** in someone else's life experience. Realizing this to be true for me, I wrote a few short lines, in two sections, which I will share with you. These lines I recite each day at the beginning of my day. I remember this almost every morning, and if I should forget, I would catch it a little later.

I am inviting you to look at these two daily thoughts and adopt one for yourself. Once you have adopted one, I am also encouraging you to think of it each day before you face your daily activities. This will help to add meaning to your day.

Before I place before you the two daily thoughts, I will share a challenge. Here we go.

Today is your day.
It will never come again.
So be a blessing.
Be a friend.
Encourage someone.
Take time to care.
Let your words heal and not hurt.

Lord, bless me today, that I may bless someone.
Give me life, that I may help someone experience a better life.
Connect with me, that I may connect with someone for You.
May the air I breathe give life to someone.
May my life today help someone experience a better life.
May I connect with someone who has been longing for a connection.

Connecting your life with either of these daily thoughts will add meaning to your life, and you will have something to look forward to each day. Please look forward to your daily experiences and enjoy what comes.

Who Is Waiting?

*The journey of life is to be experienced by you and you alone.
But the journey is for you and someone walking beside you.
For we are not made to walk alone.
And when we walk alone, we cry alone.*

There were four boys in my family. I was the youngest and treasured it. We grew up poor but did our best to give one another what we had, which was love as we understood it. As it happened in most families, there are favorites. And Venardo, the second child, was my favorite. This became more true after my two other brothers had died. Venardo and I had spent many treasured moments together in Jamaica and in Toronto, Canada.

In the middle of building more memories, Venardo was diagnosed with Alzheimer's disease. And painfully I watched him drift away from me. But even during this time, he did little things that told me that he loved me. I am about to tell you of one scene I dearly remember.

Lynn and I were taking him to a restaurant for lunch. I stopped the car close to the entrance of the restaurant to shorten the distance he would walk, since walking had become an issue and Lynn had to help him. He was helped from the car onto the sidewalk, and Lynn intended to walk him slowly to the restaurant, while I would park the car and join them later. But my dear brother would not budge from where he was dropped off.

Lynn said she encouraged him to start walking, but without success. In a few words, he made it very clear, he was **waiting** for me, his favorite brother. I joined them after parking the car, and there, standing right where I dropped them, were my brother and Lynn. He would not take a step. He was *waiting* for me. Dear reader, years later, this scene still wells up in me, tears and emotions.

Then this propels the question to you: **Who is waiting** for you? Or whom are you *waiting* for? On this journey of life with all its challenges and broken hearts, you need someone who loves you so much and cares so much to wait for you. Oh yes, I know that there are variety of ways of saying "I love you. I care." And any way is acceptable and appreciated, but there needs to be a way.

My brother is gone, and I still have that need. I want to know that there is someone *waiting* for me. Something tells me I am not alone. There are many on this journey, with the same longing and question: **who is waiting** for me?

I am walking away from this conversation with two questions for us. Please give them serious attention.

Who is waiting for you?

Whom are you *waiting* for?

The Life That Lifts

We have not lived nor are we ready to die until someone said about us, "I am who I am because of you."

Kneeling over a pile of dirt in my garden on a Sunday morning is where I found myself. And there my mind wandered to where life had taken me and to where I was. It was obvious that I would not have been there had it not been for my Creator. He knew me so well and what I would become. We worked together, and today I am pleased to tell you that my journey is successful and I am thankful and happy.

But what I really want to tell you is there are a few individuals who contributed to my life to whom I am forever grateful. I am firstly taking you to Jamaica, my birthplace.

There was Roy Osborne, who was blessed with a car and I had none, not even a driver's license, for I was just a poor teenager. But when I traveled to high school fourteen miles away, with no transportation and no money and hoped for a free lift, it was Roy who, many, many mornings, willingly and joyfully stopped and offered me a ride. I never had to ask; he just knew I needed a ride and pulled up beside me. And I jumped in and off we went. Today, when I see a hitchhiker, my heart is touched and I remember Roy's kindness. And I wished I could stop and offer a ride. I know that every time I feel this way, it is because of what Roy taught me, kindness. I am so thankful to you, Mr. Osborne. I am who I am because of you. You contributed to my journey, not only rides to school, but the lesson on kindness.

I called Roy Osborne to thank him for his kindness, and I cried as I told him the story.

There are many individuals who contributed to my journey. For example, my wife, Lynn, family, friends, and teachers, but there would not be enough pages in this book to contain the stories. But please allow me to share just three scenes.

Back to Jamaica, there was Winston Miller. He owned a new motorcycle, a Honda. Often, we rode together on his bike to his workplace in Saint Ann's Bay. Arriving there, he stepped off his bike and I slipped into the rider's seat, and off I went until the end of his workday. This was unbelievable. Every so often when I met Winston in California, I reminded him of his unusual kindness to me. Brother Win, you taught me kindness.

Sister Winnie, my dear cousin who lived in Miami, Florida, died in December 2015. For years, I called her almost every week, once or twice each week. She was my encourager. When I was a little down, she encouraged me and reminded me of how special I was. She believed that I could accomplish any task and could not be a failure. I miss her encouragement, and I have learned the importance of encouragement. I miss Sister Winnie.

My godfather, Leo B. Scott, a businessman in Saint Ann's Bay, Jamaica, died several years ago. But what he did for me will live as long as I live. You see, I, not growing up with a biological father, found myself in Scotty's life and family. He entrusted his business to me. He showed me he had confidence in me. He allowed me to handle responsible positions. He made me feel important and significant. We did things together. And I loved him so much and miss him dearly. Yes, I am who I am today because of him.

Whose life have you lifted? Who is better off because of you?

A Most Beautiful Thing

We are attracted to beauty.
It looks good.
It smells good.
It sounds good.
It makes us feel good.

One of the ***most beautiful things*** we can do for one another is to be kind. And it doesn't cost a thing.

In recent times, I have been travelling to different parts of the world for different reasons. On these trips, I often engage individuals in conversations about life. Oh yes, they have much to say about what is happening all over the world, dealing with politics, religion, family, socializations, human relations, finances, sports, entertainment, and the list continues. As I listened, I would walk away with a sense that people were deeply concerned about human relations, how we get along with one another. Is this true for you?

A pastor and I were in conversation about my coming to his church to do one of my seminars on Building Positive Relationships. He was looking forward to this seminar coming to his church. I was touched by one statement he made, so simple and yet so profound. Here it is: "I am glad you are coming to teach my people how to be KIND to one another."

"Be KIND to one another." Does this statement say anything to you? It does so much to me. It rings and sinks deeply into my passion. My heart hurts, and I feel an urgency to bring this to the attention of our civilization. Why? Because, life brings so much challenges to our everyday existence." Some of us are carrying too much, others enough. And we are longing for a break, a lift, a little KINDNESS.

I am suggesting that KINDNESS is a medicine, energy pill, cool drink, friend, warm fuzzy, sunrise, beauty, friend coming home, and the list continues. What I meant to communicate is KINDNESS makes one feel good and beautiful inside. And the great news is most KIND deeds cost nothing. Sometimes, a KIND deed is simply giving a word of encouragement. Or it might be a smile, listening, or understanding one's point of view.

For others, it might be opening a door, offering a drink of water, bringing a few tomatoes from your home garden, if you have one. There is a long list of KIND deeds we can all give away. And if only we could measure the impact of KINDNESS, maybe more of us would desire to give it away more frequently and to more people.

I am inviting you to give serious consideration to KINDNESS and what it can do and who needs it most. Please remember, we can break a whole series of tragedies with one single small KIND deed. We have it to give, so let us give it away, generously, for there are enough people who need it and are longing for it.

Be KIND. Others need it and love it. And so do we.

LIFE'S DRY POWDER

When life hands you dry powder
Add water and make a drink
When someone hands you a lemon
Add sugar and water and make lemonade

It was at the age of seven when I first thought of what I wanted to become when I grew up. I remember drawing cars, especially Jaguars, and land scenes, so I was encouraged to become an artist. A few years later, I switched to wanting to become a doctor. At the age of twelve, I changed to wanting to become a minister and began working toward that goal. I worked and worked until I achieved my goal.

The journey was very challenging. There were so many roadblocks and impassable lanes, but God's power, love, direction, my family's help, and my self-determination—these propelled me forward, and I was successful in reaching my goal.

Many of us have dreams and goals. And have seen successes and failures. I am celebrating with you the successes. But what about the failures, the broken dreams, and disappointments? I imagine that these have resulted in agitation, discouragement, brokenness, tears, sleepless nights, blue and cloudy days. I am sorry you had to walk these paths. But I have great news for anyone walking in these experiences. You do not have to live in them nor be held a prisoner in them. Like a baby, when he/she falls, there is the looking around a bit, rising, and walking again to the goal. The disappointed adult not only rises and walks, but *when handed dry powder, adds water and makes a drink, and when handed a lemon, makes lemonade.*

This means, when we lose a job, this might be the opportunity to find a better job, retrain, or just move into a completely different work field. When plan B fails, then it is time to work on plan D. We have the capability to turn disadvantages into advantages, a bad situation into a good situation, sadness into laughter, night into day.

I remotely remember a story about a farming experience in Alabama, where there was a very bad cotton failure one year, which drove the farmers to try peanuts the next year, which was a tremendous success. (I am subject to correction on this story.)

When your field fails you, why not try another product? Maybe the field is ripe for this. When you fall, don't just sit there. Time is lost while sitting. Rise immediately and walk. Embrace and celebrate the opportunity to do something different or meet someone different.

Ice Cream Cone

Our value is measured by our usefulness
How we interface with our environment
And how other lives are colored
By who we are
So let us live with others
With the good life in mind
And how shall we live?

Stretch beyond yourself
Believe in yourself
Help one in need
Meet new people
Be inspirational
Be encouraging
Keep the cool
Like yourself
Be positive
Have fun
Keep fit
Be fun
Laugh
Live

(The construction of the above characteristics is in the shape of an ice cream cone. Thus when I refer to ice cream cone, I am referring to these characteristics.)

When we open our eyes each day and see the beauty of the day, let us give thanks for all we have and for what we do not have.

For what we have are the special gifts to contribute to the good life. And what we do not have are those conditions which cause limitations to our lives, those conditions which cause pain. And the list is long.

We are not taking time to focus on those limitations. Instead, we will focus on those conditions which contribute to the good life for us and for those within our circle.

All around us, each day, there are individuals who love life like we do and who are hoping that who we are and what we do or say will brighten their day and give meaning to their lives. They realize they cannot do it alone; they cannot walk the lonely, painful path alone. They are looking to us to come by, be nice and assuring. Be an ***ice cream cone.***

Within this ***ice cream cone*** are several characteristics which can contribute to the good life for us and those within our circle. Have as much as our lives can hold, and please let us remember to share, for there are others looking on and waiting for their portion. And if we do not share, who will?

Every One an Angel

Lord, bless me today that I may bless someone for you.
Give me life that I may help someone experience a better life.
Connect with me that I may connect with someone for you.

Many of us have a routine with which we begin our day. I have a routine to which I try to be faithful. At the beginning of each day, and several times during my busy day, I take time to talk to God, using the language above, "Lord, bless me today . . ."

One Monday morning, about thirty minutes after making this request to God to bless me that day, my telephone rang. It was a business friend from far away, Jamaica. We talked about some business matters, and at the end of our conversation, I, without any reason, asked her if she had anything she wanted to tell me. She was silent. Then I repeated the question. "Do you have anything you want to tell me?" It is not my habit to ask that question, especially when she had not indicated she was having any difficulties. Then she slowly opened her heart to me. I sensed she was nervous as she explained what was happening in her life. Her concern was very important to her. So when she was through, I assured her that her concern was heard and would be given further thought. So after Lynn and I looked at the situation, I called my business friend and told her that we wanted to be involved in her situation. Oh, my friend began to cry and flooded the air with thankfulness. (Let us call her Sadie.)

It then came to my attention that thirty minutes earlier, I had asked that I would be used to make someone happy. This was the instant answer.

The next day, Sadie called me, and we talked more about her situation. I deeply felt her sense of gratitude because we cared for her situation. And in her tearful voice she said to me: "I have an ***angel*** in Oregon." Yes, she was referring to Lynn and me, since we live in Oregon.

Truly, it was our delight to have heard Sadie's concern and responded from a heart that cared. As I sensed Sadie's joys, I too became extra joyful. But I also know that Lynn and I are not the only ***angels.*** You are also an ***angel***, in your own way. For you too have a caring heart. You too want to make someone happy. You too have caringly entered into someone's situation, which led to a sea of gratitude. Sometimes, we are ***angels*** and do not know.

I am happy for you and all who take the time to be ***angels***.

God bless you, ***angel***. And to Sadie, my friend in Jamaica, to you I say, "You are my Jamaican ***angel***."

Turbulence

When I'm flying to my favorite vacation spot and the plane begins to shake because of turbulence, I'm staying in my seat and fasten my seat belt. I'm not getting off.

I still remember my first airplane flight from Jamaica to Toronto, Canada. I was thrilled to be going to Canada, but getting there was a pain. I heard every sound, every closed door, every bump along the way, and I suffered, because no one had prepared me. No one told me there could be **turbulence** along the way.

Since then, June, 16, 1966, I have made several airplane journeys. My longest trips were to the Philippines and to South Africa and many trips to Jamaica and other parts of North America. I am pleased to tell you that I am no more bothered by the bangs from the closed doors, not even the bumps along the way. I have learned to expect these, for they are the natural experiences of flying by plane.

Looking back on those bumpy flights and banging doors that sounded like the plane was falling apart, I asked myself the question, "What would have happened if I had decided to open the door of the plane and jumped out?" If you think this question is ridiculous, you are right. But the wise thing I learned was when there was **turbulence**, I listened to the pilot and buckled my seat belt. No, don't jump out. Stay on board, for soon the **turbulence** will pass. This is the wise and safe way to travel.

Those of us who have travelled by plane, at some time, surely experienced some degree of **turbulence.** But we stayed on board, rode out the storm, experienced a calmness, and safely landed. Right?

Turbulence is an expected condition on the journey of life. Let me cite a few examples. We do not always get along with our spouses. The people at work see things differently. Bosses get under our skins. A friend of many years did you wrong. These inflict ***turbulence.*** And while it might be easy to jump out, turn our backs, walk away, sometimes, this action might be as unwise as jumping from a plane during a ***turbulence***.

Recently, I was distressed about the behavior of an organization of which I am a member. And I thought of jumping out. I said to myself, "I don't need this. Let them handle it their way." But then I remembered my airplane flight experiences of ***turbulence.*** So I decided that the right response was to stay with the organization and work with it. I can help on board, and not while I am falling to my death.

So if you are experiencing a ***turbulence*** at home, at work, at school, with a friend or relationship, in life's journey, please buckle up, stay on board. This too will pass and soon you will land safely.

Happy flight to you, even in ***turbulence.***

HERE AND NOW

*There is no moment bigger than now. So whatever your
hands find to do, do it now, for then may never come.*

Lynn and I were privileged to be on a cruise where I did a seminar for a group of church leaders. This was my first cruise, and there were so many things I took away from this experience. But there was one I especially cherished and will share with you.

Just before we disembarked, we met one of the hosts named Jamuna. She was exceptional in the way she greeted and related to us. She made us feel so welcomed and comfortable, and I wanted to spend more time in her presence. While enjoying our time with her, I said to her, "Jamuna, you know what, you are bigger than this ship." She got my message. For what I wanted her to know was she had relational talents which should go beyond working on a cruise ship. She was that good and effective, I thought.

Days later, as I remembered my cruise experiences and thought of Jamuna and my words to her, I decided to reconsider what I said to her. For even though I might have been correct in my assessment, maybe it needed some modification. And this is the reason for writing this experience, so please hear me out.

Jamuna was excellent as host on this cruise. Then, what made me think that she would be equally excellent elsewhere?

It is possible that being on this cruise ship is the place for her.

In our progressive society, we are known to take good people and relocate them only to destroy them. They would have been better serving where they were. It is true, there are ladders to climb and opportunities where we can become better. But there are times when we are better, growing right where we are. For that's where we were destined to be. That was why I later thought that maybe Jamuna would do her best on the cruise ship.

This introduces the next thought. The grass is not green only out there. It is green right here where we are. We don't have to wait for tomorrow to do something good. We can do it today. We don't have to wait for the big moment. Every moment is an opportunity, and that might be the big moment and the only one we will ever get. We don't have to wait for tomorrow; we can do it now, **here and now.** For tomorrow may never come. Some people have a friend named Procrastination. Others have a friend named "I am waiting for the right opportunity."

What I am reminding you of is this, or; Whatever your plans are, implement them **here and now**. There is a child to help, a neighbor to encourage, a staff member to compliment, a family member to love. Please don't wait for the right place nor time, for the right place and time is right before you, created just for you, **here and now.**

Just do it and get over it. Now you can go on to other things.

MEMORIES

I would rather live with a memory than live with nothing, for memories are the works of art that bring me joy, and even when they bring me pain, I remember that there was an original joy.

It was back in the early part of 1970 when a couple friends and I, living in Toronto, Canada, went on a spiritual journey. On that journey we wanted to experience a more enriched prayer experience. So we decided that we would take time to pray every day at 2:00 p.m., wherever we were and whatever we were doing. Among the things I prayed for was my dear mother, who was living in Jamaica. It was like I was visiting her every day at 2:00 p.m. And I liked this. But then later Mother died, and it became hard to pray at the usual time, because circumstances had changed. I tried for a while until I finally chose to discontinue my 2:00 p.m. prayer. This was a memory which brought me pain, tears, and joy.

Then there was my favorite brother living in Toronto, Canada. I looked forward to calling him every Sunday. We had so much to talk about and sometimes nothing. Having lost my parents and two other brothers and since he was the only one left, our time together was very special. Sundays became special to me. But then he died and I could no longer call him, and all I am left with are **memories.**

Then there was one of my favorite cousins who lived in Miami, Florida. She and I were close. We spent special times together, especially when we lived in Jamaica. Once we reconnected after she moved to Miami, I telephoned her almost every Saturday morning. I called her while Lynn and I were on our way to church. This was something to which I looked forward to. But then she died, and I no longer was able to call her. And now I am left with only *memories*.

My daughter, son, and family are living not too far from us. We attempt to call them on Saturday mornings on our way to church. This is our way of greeting and connecting with them. There have been a few times the call was not made, but the thought was always there. Then there were the times we did not make the call and they would call. This was nice. This is building *memories*.

I know that some *memories* bring pain, tears, joy, or hope.

Also *memories* are like vitamins. For *memories* walk into our circumstances and change things. Sometimes, when we have nothing and life is challenging, all that are left for us are *memories*.

I am encouraging you to make *memories*. Every day and every conscious moment are opportunities to make *memories*. Therefore, please let us live lives that will bear *memories* like delicious fruits. One question we are to ask ourselves is "How do we want to be remembered when we are no longer here? What *memories* do we want to leave behind?"

SHOCKING SHOPPERS

Some say life is bad.
Others say things are getting worse.
I say life is good when I see it through good people.

Lesmin told me an experience she had, and I was so touched, I am sharing it with you. For the story to have a greater impact, there are two things for you to know.

(1) Lesmin was born in Jamaica, West Indies. (2) At the time of this story, she was like any average American citizen, not showing signs of one needing help in any way.

She stopped by a supermarket to pick up a few items. At the checkout counter, there were two ladies ahead of her. Then one lady joined the line behind her. The lady behind her offered to pick up her basket and place it on the counter for her. Just then, the customer ahead of her turned and saw what had taken place, and offered to pay for Lesmin's grocery. Lesmin said she was sort of in shock. So she politely declined the offer; however, the customer insisted that Lesmin accept her offer, just to make her day.

At that point, Lesmin accepted and thanked her. The customer behind her was also shocked and said, "I have been in this supermarket over and over and have never seen this." Lesmin said that what she learned from that was "that actions are contagious negatively or positively." And what was unique about that was the two ladies, one behind her and the other in front, were of different ethnic background from Lesmin. And to this, Lesmin said, "It goes to show it's not the color of the skin as much as what's in the heart."

Yes, there are individuals in our world who are cold, mean, and indifferent. These hurt us along life's journey, and we pray that they will someday have a change of heart. On the other hand, we might have to coexist with these people and give them all the love we can, for this might be all they will ever get.

This story is not about the undesirable citizens. But what I want us to see in this story is there are still beautiful people in our world. They are kind, nice, thoughtful, and caring. We will find them in our cities, on our streets, in our stores, and where we work. They are like a flower garden, different in colors, textures, and shapes, but beautiful. And by the way, am I talking about you?

Each day, as I listen to the news and become aware of what is happening in our world, it becomes clearer and more urgent for us to pay more attention to people, those whom we live among and wherever we find them. People who live among us and even strangers are crying for respect, kindness, and tender, compassionate responses. These will affect behaviors and produce the culture we long for and the world needs. So, please give your part of niceness, and someday I might write your story like that of the ***"Shocking Shoppers."***

Be beautiful
Find beautiful people
Tell them they are beautiful
And we will be on the road to a beautiful life

The Sweeper

If a man is called to be street sweeper he should sweep streets even as Michelangelo painted, or Beethoven composed music, or as Shakespeare wrote poetry. He should sweep streets so well that all the hosts of heaven and earth will pause to say, here lived a great street sweeper who did his job well.

—Martin Luther King Jr.

I remember well, at the ages from seven to twelve, when I lived in Jamaica. My home was located high up on a hill. It was a very humble home, but from there we were able to see the blue Caribbean Sea one mile away and several other scenes added to our view. Our kitchen was located outside the house about thirty feet away. And between the house and the kitchen was a dirt section, no, not concrete pavement.

Mother had made it plain to me that it was my responsibility to keep that dirt section clean. And so every day, sometimes several times per day, I got my coconut broom that came from the coconut or palm tree and swept the area. My intent was to remove straying leaves or any undesired objects. Fortunately, I enjoyed sweeping, since this was done daily. I still remember how clean that section looked when I was finished sweeping. All the leaves were gone, and where the dirt had made a pile, it was nicely redistributed. It had looked like a work of art. I did my job and did it well. Mother was pleased and so was I.

The opportunity comes to all of us to do our best, whatever the task may be, to the extent that those around us and we ourselves will be satisfied. No, you might not be asked to sweep a dirt section, but maybe to sweep the garage, driveway, or back porch. Then it might not be to sweep, but to dust furniture, wash a car, pull weeds, care for someone, or do a task. Life is made of tasks and responsibilities. We cannot live without being surrounded by things to do. And it does matter how we care for these tasks or things to be done. When we have done our deeds and done them well and are satisfied, something happens to us, something good that makes us feel good. Therefore, whatever we set our minds to do, let us encourage our minds by doing it well. Whatever we are asked to do, once we accept the responsibility to do it, let us do it joyfully and well until we are satisfied.

Some individuals do well whatever they are called to do. They remove every hindrances and move forward. They are successful because of the following reasons: They have a passion for the task. They appropriate time to do the task. There is accountability. There is a sense of doing things to the fullest. They have a model, someone whom they admire.

I might not have mentioned the reason why you do your task well to the fullest. But whatever your reason, it is commendable that you "sweep" well. So today, I am encouraging you to continue being the great *sweeper.* For not only will you be enriched by this, but also someone might be watching you and learning from you. So "sweep" well, *sweeper*.

The Empty Seat

It may seem so important to you, but less important when you understand how important it was to someone else.

Those of you who travel by plane, especially for long hours, will be able to relate to this experience. Lynn and I were travelling from Detroit, Michigan, to Portland, Oregon. It was a night flight, and so it would be easy to sleep on this flight if all the conditions were right. For comfort, I usually sit by the aisle and Lynn would be in the center while the third passenger would sit by the window. But for a little more comfort, we would hope that there was no third passenger, which would allow Lynn to have a little spread onto the third **empty seat.** This was important to us.

On this particular flight, we were among the early ones to be seated. Passengers filed in by the dozens and went to all the seats behind us and on the other side of the plane, but no one came to our row. We were watching the line and hoping that the passengers would continue toward the back, so that Lynn and I would have the luxury of an **empty seat** in our row. Finally we saw the end of the line, and that last person was looking toward the back of the plane, not toward our seat which was toward the front. So I got Lynn's attention and began to celebrate because of **the empty seat**. But the celebration was conservative and would be until the door to the plane was closed. Then, I heard the door close. I knew the sound. Then the flight attendant formally announced that the door was closed. Now the party in my heart began, for we have beside us an **empty seat**, which meant that Lynn could stretch out and have a little more comfort on this long flight.

We relaxed for the night. Seat belts buckled, just waiting for the push back. Then there was the voice from the cockpit, which said lunches and snacks were not on the plane and we were waiting for them to arrive. It would take approximately twenty minutes. That was fine; we could wait. But then while we waited, something surprising happened; a fine-looking young man was walking down the aisle and looking toward my row. Yes, he stopped by my row and headed for *the empty seat* by the window.

What happened? He was late for this flight and would have to make other arrangements, most likely take another flight the next day. But because we were waiting for the food delivery, he was allowed on this flight. Yes, I was disappointed. Yes, I wished I did not lose the luxury of *the empty seat*. But later I reflected and wondered what that passenger would have missed had the plane left. Would his family be disappointed? Would he miss an important appointment the next day? Had he been travelling and tired and was anxious to sleep in his own bed? While I was disappointed about losing *the empty seat*, was he delighted to fill *the* **empty seat**?

After the reflection, I realized that my disappointment was someone else's delight. And that life was not all about me, but the other person.

Tell Me More

*Everyone has a story to tell and wants to tell.
Our gift to someone is to give the opportunity to tell that story.*

It was very obvious that Kevin was hurting as he stood there looking at the picture of his dead buddy. Being aware of what he might be going through, I stepped closer to him and said, "Tell me more." It was amazing the transformation that came over him. He repositioned himself to a position of confidence, ease, and enlightenment. Then he began to tell the story of their friendship. Yes, the whole atmosphere had changed, for Kevin wanted to talk about his buddy. And I had just opened the door, and he let the story out.

Lynn and I were vacationing in Hawaii when we walked onto the beach for our day's walk. Standing by a monument was a man paying intense attention to the inscription as if he was reading this for the first time. We asked about the monument, to learn that it was about his best buddy who had died there in the ocean. And that this man visited the site daily. We asked some questions and gave this man the opportunity to talk. He opened his heart to us, and we felt he wanted to talk about his buddy.

I was shopping in Safeway store by the fruit stand. The gentleman standing across from me admired the Hawaiian shirt I was wearing. I accepted his compliment and inquired if he had ever visited Hawaii. His countenance lighted when he said yes and that he was there during the war and that he had been in the service all over the world. I had opened the door for him to tell me about his life, and he took the opportunity to **tell me more.**

Dear Vashti was hospitalized for multiple medical conditions. She had been there before, and here she was again. So you can imagine what was going on in her mind. On top of that she had just received news that morning about a test she recently had, and the news was bad. Again, imagine how she is feeling.

And now here I walk into her hospital room. What will I say? What can I say? I have been in this situation several times, and there is no textbook answer as to what to say at a moment like this. But I did not need to push Vashti to talk. She volunteered some information, and then came my opportunity to say, "Vashti, please ***tell me more.***" Her countenance seemed to have changed; her posture became more confident. And she took it away. She told me more stories, stories close to her heart.

As we interconnect with people, maybe the best gift we can offer them is the opportunity for them to tell their stories. People have stories to tell and love to tell them. When we open the door, they will open their minds. It is simple to say, "Vashti, ***tell me more***."

Let us be sure we mean it and take time to listen to the stories.

Dog Biscuits

Be kind for everyone you meet is fighting a battle.

—John Watson

Some people repel dogs. They are cold to dogs, and those dogs know that and react negatively. It has been my observation that if you hate a dog, it will hate you, and if you love a dog, it will love you. But I am sure we all know of the exceptions, and I am about to introduce an exception to you.

Our neighbors had just moved into the home across the fence from us. It is a cyclone fence with climbing rose bushes, and our neighbors and we do see what is happening on both sides of the fence. This is not a problem. We are both warm and friendly neighbors. But there was one problem. The problem was they own two dogs. I am inviting you to meet one of the dogs, Marley.

Firstly, you need to know that I have had a positive history with dogs. I have been in challenging situations where I could have been eaten by dogs, but where one dog escorted me to the door of the home. Dogs and I are friends. But not this time. Marley was not sure about me. She growled most ferociously whenever we are in contact. I feared her growls and really appreciated a reliable fence between us.

Our neighbor, sensing the battle and my good intentions, offered me some **dog biscuits** and suggested that I reach out to Marley with these biscuits. Then the miracle began. Marley cautiously drew closer and closer and warmer and warmer as I reached out to her with **dog biscuits**.

Now, Marley is my friend. Not just mine, but Lynn's also. This is what you will see if you are looking at our relationships: When Marley hears my back door open, she rushes to the fence, and in a praying position she waits for her treat from me, ***dog biscuits***. If I am slow acknowledging her, she will let me know she is there. She sees me through our back glass door and will sit waiting for me. She follows me from one end of the fence to the other. When I am working in the backyard, she sits there, keeping me company, and this could be for an hour or more. Sometimes, I forget about her being there, until I move, and then there is a rush to my new position. Marley is my friend. Our relationship is founded on ***dog biscuits***.

You and I are constantly interacting with individuals who do not share our styles, and frictions do form. And so we wish things were different and wish we could get along. Sometimes we are successful, and other times, we are not. There are still growling and ferocious connections. My question is have we tried ***dog biscuits?*** Surely, you know what I mean. Have we tried kindness, deeds of kindness? It worked for Marley and me. Maybe, it will work for you.

I plead with you, my reader, to commit yourself to each day, breathe a little kindness to your contacts. For more than ever, our world needs ***dog biscuits*** (kindness).

RESTORATION

A little deed of kindness takes little time, but makes a mountain.

    I stopped by the Dollar Store to secure an item. In the checkout line, just behind me was a lady. I invited her to go in front of me, but she refused. She indicated that she had to go to her car for some money, so it was all right for me to go first. So she left her goodies on the counter and began to walk to her car for some money. I caught her attention and asked her how much money she was short. She said it was only fifty cents. I offered to give her the fifty cents, and she came back and joined the checkout line. I further offered to pay for the few items she had. She was shocked and exclaimed, "Thank you. You are such a gentleman. You restore my faith in humanity. For there are so many things happening in the world these days."

    I thanked her for her kind words, and I walked away from the store, thinking of how a very small deed and a few cents can change and impact a person. I do not remember how much I paid for the lady's goods, but I know it was less than two dollars. So now I am thinking that lady's views about the world has been changed by less than two dollars. Now her faith was **restored in humanity** because of a simple deed I did.

    What is true is we do not know what people are dealing with, what is happening in their lives. It was possible that that lady had a bad experience with someone recently. Possibly, her respect for the world was tarnished and maybe would hesitate to trust or believe in people. And at the right time, I was placed at the Dollar Store to give her a different perspective of people. One never knows.

Then I was driven to look back at the part I played. It was my opportunity to invite the lady to step in front of me, to offer to make up the difference in what she was short in change, and to pay for all her groceries. These opportunities do come by, and it is good to be aware of them. And just think, all it cost me was even less than two dollars. It is amazing that two dollars can change a situation and a person.

Not all opportunities involve money, and that is a good thing, for not all of us can afford additional expenses. But there are so many opportunities out there to connect with someone and make a difference. There are so many little things we can do. We can do any of these: say hello, smile, allow someone to go first, open a door, say thanks, pay for a treat for a little kid, pick up an item someone dropped, give a compliment, and the list continues. And we will never know what effect our actions will have. Really, it is not for us to know. What really matters is that we become passionate about doing kind deeds to those who need them. It is a really great thing to have a passion to be kind and nice. This makes one feel good and makes the world feel good and could restore a good feeling about humanity.

So the next time you are out, please be sensitive about what nice, kind thing you can do for someone. And remember, it might come back to you, even sooner than you can imagine.

How about us being about the business of **restoration**? **Restoring** people and their values and what is important to them and the world?

The Little Things

It is often the tiniest of gestures that make the MOST difference.

—Anonymous

  Looking through my pile of papers, a little piece of paper containing this message popped up before me. I made several attempts to discard it, but the message came pouncing on me. "It is the little things that matter." So I decided to bring this to your table.

  In one of my previous books, *A Quiet Place*, is a section titled **"The Little Things."** And from this section, I am giving you just a taste.

  One evening while at the church, Debbie said she had something for me. She had gone to Portland that day. Remembering my delight, she brought for me a delicious slice of carrot cake, with even a fork. Thanks, Debbie.

  She must have heard that I enjoyed ginger drinks. So one Sabbath morning, she stopped in my office with a gift for me. It was a bottle of ginger drink. Thanks, Linda.

  My invitation to you is to take the opportunity to do a ***little thing*** for someone. It might be returning a cart to the cart rack at the shopping center. It might be opening a door for a teenager. It might be sending a card to a friend. It might be shopping for a surprise gift for a family member, or it might be just a smile or encouragement.

  You will never know what your ***little thing*** will do, and you do not need to know, so just try it someday.

  In addition to what I have shared from my book, here are some other examples of the ***little things***:

I stopped by the bank to take care of some business. As many bank personnel do, there was a warm stream of greetings extended to me. But the one that touched most was one teller reached out and offered me one candy. It was as if she had just given me a piece of her heart.

There was another bank in my city where when I walked in there was also a stream of warm greetings. But on this particular day, one of the bank personnel walked away from her desk and, from behind the counter, met me in the lobby, just to say hello and to connect.

Driving along the main street in town, I saw a police car travelling the opposite direction. I waved, and so did the driver. Shortly after the wave, I turned in a business complex, just to observe that the police car was following me. I stopped and stepped out. The police car pulled up beside me and stopped. I recognized the officer, and so we greeted. To my amazement, he said, "I just wanted to say hello." Wow!

She and I were entering the church building at the same time. I hurried ahead in order that I may open the door for her. And I did. She expressed appreciation and added, "Oh, how I love your smile."

I drove onto the parking lot of the grocery store, and there was a lady standing by her car as if she was in trouble, maybe her battery had died. So I circled and pulled up beside her and asked if everything was all right. She said she was fine, just waiting for her brother. She was so amazed that I stopped for her and said she felt like crying.

My dominant colors for church that day was purple. He too was wearing purple, and so he came close to me to highlight our colors and requested that a picture be taken of us. He said we were brothers. Great. **The little things** matter.

LIFESAVERS

Every day they put their lives on the line.

    You may consider it unusual for me to include this portion in my book. But from the very depth of my heart, I want to write this for you and all the world. The thoughts included in this portion are not unique and mine alone. So I want to join other like-minded individuals to write about a very important family. This family is the law enforcement men and women who serve us in our cities, on our highways, in our shopping malls, at our airports, and wherever there are people. These men and women are often referred to as the ones who put their lives on the line. Therefore I call them **lifesavers.** You will agree that it is worth watering the plants that bring us vegetables. For this reason, I write these thoughts.

    There are bad cops, and we will find them in many places. These bad cops might not be bad though. They might be misguided and possess shattered emotions, which get away from them under pressure. To them we are to extend our prayers and love. For love and prayers change people and circumstances. Now, please come with me to my city, Woodburn, in Oregon, USA. Please take a peep at the policemen and women here, with whom I often interact.

    My dearest brother living in Toronto, Canada, had just died, and I had just returned from his funeral. A broken heart and shattered emotions had overwhelmed me while driving from the post office. And there in front of me was a police officer on his bike. I knew who he was, so I followed him for several turns. He stopped in a parking lot, and I pulled up beside him. And I just opened my brokenness to him. He gave me what he could, and I felt better. He is my friend forever.

Driving along the main street in town, I saw a police car travelling the opposite direction. I waved, and so did the driver. Shortly after our waves, I turned into a business complex, just to observe that the police car had made a U-turn and was following me. I stopped and stepped out. The police car pulled up beside me and stopped. I recognized the officer, and so we greeted. To my amazement he said, "I just wanted to say hello." Wow!

Driving by the police station, I noted that there was a police car turning in at the station. So, I turned in ahead of him and stopped. The car followed me and stopped beside me. We both stepped out of our vehicles, greeted, and hugged as we usually do. We shared some thoughts about life, and he reached into his pocket and then came closer to me and placed something into my outer jacket pocket. I was scared to look, so as soon as it was convenient, I peeped into the envelope, expecting to find a sticker like what is often given to kids. But no, it was not a sticker. To my surprise, it was a gift card to STARBUCKS. Wow! But this is not all. A couple of days later, I received a text from that same police officer, saying he wanted to be sure that I had his personal cell phone number. Yes, we are friends. Thanks, friend, and all you who **put your lives on the line** for us. You are our *lifesavers.* We appreciate you, and we thank you.

WHAT YOU DID NOT WANT

Don't judge the book by its cover.

—*Anonymous*

    This was my first time visiting the doctor's office. There were several attendants assisting patients. As particular as I am, I wondered who would be assisting me and determined that it would not be "that one." Moments later, my name was called, and I was relieved for it was not "that one." So I sat at the desk and was answering questions when, guess who walked over to my desk? "That one" whom we will name Gill.

    She volunteered to assist the one who was assigned to me and soon took over, for she was more experienced. I began to admire her skills at the job and enjoy her warm personality. She was pleasant and even encouraged a conversation of interest to me. I was liking this experience. At the end of that session, I told her that when I returned to this office, I would ask for her. And can you believe it, the next times I went to that doctor's office, I was sure to ask for Gill.

    At my next visits, Gill was just as nice, and I told her that she was a nice person. She replied that she was a Christian lady and tried to be nice to everyone. She was truly successful at being a nice Christian person.

    During one of our conversations, Gill learned that I was a Christian. She asked where I went to church, and when I told her, she alarmingly indicated that one of her friends attended my church. Now we both knew the same person. And that drew me even closer to her. For you see, we shared an appreciation for Christianity, we shared the same friend, and now we were on the way to build our own friendship.

Looking back, I felt disappointed with myself for being so prejudiced toward someone whom I did not even know. That was not fair nor nice. And again I learned, **"Don't judge the book by its cover."** Don't judge people by how they look, or even what I think of them, for inside, they might be a jewel.

What is interesting is I have had similar experiences at other times. Gill's situation was not my first, nor was it the last. I am constantly faced with the temptation to prejudge people. From a distance, I know whether they are nice or not, without giving them a fair chance. Do you know what I mean?

Gill's situation is constantly before me, and I am learning and growing to accept all people. Treating them all nicely and fairly. Nurturing the relationship and allowing it to become a garden of fruitful produce. I am aware that most of the people I encounter share different values and styles. But rather than spotlighting the differences, I am learning to celebrate those areas where we are alike. It is a matter of covering the darkness with light, or adding sugar to a drink that is bitter.

I do not want to miss the opportunities of being with someone who is nice because of my prejudiced attitude. Neither do I want to wrongfully spill ugliness on someone because of my prejudiced attitude. I want to see the beauty in people and return the appropriate response. I want to taste the pie before I throw it away. What do you say?

JUST FOR TODAY

It is the little tweet of the little bird
It is the sweet song from the lips of the little girl
It is the smile of a mother
Or the laughter of the baby in the crib
It is whatever you have to give
That might make all the difference
So whatever you have to give me
I will gladly accept it

Today, I am giving you my friendship
In times like these, friendship is beautiful
I am giving you my heart
And as you process each challenge
Just know that my friendship
Closes in beside you
And my heart is beating beside yours

I am singing for you
I am planting flowers for you
I am waving my arms
In order to create a still breeze around you
I am spreading my wings
In order to form sheltering clouds over you

And I am spreading my coat for you to walk on
To keep the shine on your shoes
Then look ahead and there is the sunrise

Look behind, there is the moon

And in the shadow is a little quiet smile
From me to you
Just to tell you
That everything is going to be all right.

From what I have been reading lately and from what others have been telling me and from my own personal experiences, what people are longing for mostly is someone to care. Someone to understand. Someone to give a kind word and a word of hope. Tell them that everything is going to be all right and you will be with them when time gets rough. Tell them that time will get rough, but they will not be alone. And, dear reader, when you make such promise, please be faithful to your promise. Be there when times get rough, and even when times are good, be there.

We are not to spend too much time figuring out what might we do to keep a friend afloat who might be sinking. Just throw an object to hang on to. Sometimes, it does not really matter what that object might be, so long as it is floatable.

Then there are the other times when a friend is sitting at home lonely and worried about the unknown, what tomorrow might bring. At these times, we may never know what our friend needs most, and it is then when the little things may be the answer. Oh yes, the little things which may bring a smile, revive a pleasant memory or paint a line of hope.

We never know what will work for our friends. We only know that something will work. And how? Neither do we know. So as we live today, let it be our attitude to give jewels away. They may save a life.

Turn Right and Go Straight

Plant a tree
Leave it to grow
You never know how many fruits it will produce
Nor who will eat from it

    Many years ago, in the year 1964, I attended what was then West Indies College in Mandeville, Jamaica. I was just a young man desirous of becoming a minister. Sometime there, a guest preacher had come to the college for what we called Week of Prayer, which was a week of spiritual awakening and development. As I recall, several times during the week, the guest preacher used the words ***"turn right and go straight."*** He was admonishing us students to change our course, the direction we were going, and turn right. And after we have turned right, go straight. Keep going straight. Do not turn to the right nor to the left nor turn back.

    Well, that admonition, ***"turn right and go straight"*** must have had tremendous impact on me, because I grafted it into my young preaching life. Let me explain. Way back there, between 1964 and 1965, I preached a sermon in my hometown, in the town square. In that sermon, I admonished the crowd to change their ways, ***"turn right and go straight."*** My wife, Lynn, told me she remembered me using that sentence, ***"Turn right and go straight."*** And this would have been many years later, after I used it in my town in Jamaica.

    Now, why is this coming to life again? I do want you to know, so here I go.

    On Tuesday, April 11, 2017, I attended my elementary school reunion in Jamaica. Alvin Williams, a past student and the assembly speaker for that morning, challenged the students to set their goals high and follow their goals to the very end. He told them a story about a young man, many years ago, who in the town square admonished the gathering to *"turn right and go straight."* And that the young man was Mr. Ewart F. Brown. (That was me.) Alvin told the students that his life was successful because of that statement, *"Turn right and go straight."* When I heard that from Alvin, strange emotions welled up inside of me. Did one statement from me actually give direction to someone? According to Alvin, yes, it did. And I am so glad for this. In fact, I have observed and heard Alvin as he motivated other gatherings, and I have been very impressed by him. And now, just think, one statement from me played a part in his development. Wow!

My message behind this story is to alert us that what we say can make a difference. Each word counts. Each sentence counts.

And we never know who is listening and who will fly away to change the world, to make this place better. Alvin Williams, now living in Florida and a successful banker now retired, took my words seriously and changed his personal world and still changing others even today. Thanks, Alvin, and congratulations to you. God bless you.

And now to you, dear reader, I say, if your direction needs alteration, *"turn right and go straight."*

A Daily Prayer

Dear God
Make me useful today
Give me a purpose to live
May it be
To share the joy of life
Make me porous
That fresh air will flow through me to others

This morning after I saw the sunshine and did the necessary morning chores, it was necessary to have a conversation with Mari. During our conversation, I saw the opportunity to give her some words of encouragement and affirmation. She received them well. And I was glad I gave them. I experienced an amazing delight from how she responded to the affirmations. Again, it became clear to me that when you give goodie affirmations, and when they are followed by positive responses, it returns goodie good feelings to you, the giver. Now two people are fed and happy, both Mari and I.

I am going to tell you about my meeting with a lady at Fred Meyer's store. As I walked through the front entrance, there was a lady sitting on a chair. I had never before seen a worker sitting on a chair by the main entrance. She caught my attention, because of her posture on the chair. She sat very straight and seemed uncomfortable. I stopped, greeted her, and we exchanged a few words. And then she paused and said to me, "May I ask you a favor?"

"Surely, you can" was my response.

Then she asked, "Can you help me up?"

Oh my, I was shocked at this, for I have been asked many favors but never one like this, especially coming from a stranger. So I gladly seized the privilege and positioned myself beside her, and she held on to me and raised herself to a standing position. She said she needed to go for a walk to get some fresh air.

She was on her way outside for fresh air and I continued inside the store, but she was on my mind, and I hoped I would see her on my way out. Surely, there she was back on her chair. Again we exchanged some thoughts. She indicated that she was dealing with some personal issues, and as she unloaded her brokenness, my heart was shaken. I realized that, that Friday morning was given to me for that lady. It was not an accident that I ran into her, but there was a reason. As we continued talking and I assured her that she was valuable to society and to God, she was hesitant to accept my kindness, while her face was bathed with tears. I gave her reasons to believe that she was special and valuable, and a smile emerged through her tears. And as I said goodbye to her, she said to me, "You are nice." And my heart cried.

It has been my experience that along with all the many things I have to accomplish each day, it is well to remember that there are people around me who are hurting and would appreciate a little touch of love and attention. I want to so live each day that there will be time to make a difference in someone's life, to brighten someone's gloomy day. How about you?

WHAT I LEFT BEHIND

*It is not all about what you brought to the table.
It is also about what you left behind on the table.*

Dave and I have met previously to discuss some business interests because he has a sharp business mind. On this day, he and I again were in conversation about a business matter. He gave me some sound business directions, which I very much appreciated. I expressed to him a mountain of thanks, and I left his office feeling great and ready to move ahead toward success.

But just a few minutes after I left his presence, something came over me. I cannot recall having this feeling or thought in recent times. I focused on what had just come over me, to the extent that it troubled me and made me decide to share it with you. It can best be told in this question, "What message did I leave behind?" In other words, "What was Dave thinking of me after I left his presence?"

Is this question important? What does it matter what others think of me? Isn't it true that all that matters is that I live my life and live it the best way I know and let the chips fall wherever?

Let me suggest that the question about the influence of my life is important. It does matter what others think of me. It does matter how my living affects others. You see, we are here in this life for one another. We were designed to be a community and family. And when we cohabitate the same space, culture, or values, we are inclined to become what we live with. We either become similar or dissimilar, and this may be by osmosis or by intentional choices. For when we observe a behavior, we may choose to follow that pattern of living or choose to resent that behavior.

It is a solemn responsibility that falls on us to be a school where others learn how to live. And while it is a solemn responsibility, it is also a privilege. For our way of living could be the reason for one's choice of career, choice of a companion, choice of clothes and dress, and just a multitude of choices. Some of us may live to know of how we might have influenced others while others may never know. And for those who never know, it really does not matter if we know. If only we could just know that someone is a success or a better person because of our way of living.

Recently, I was in conversation with a friend from college, and it was a delight. I told her of her father, who was my mentor and hero. It was because of him, Pastor Silburn Reid, that I, at the age of twelve, chose to become a minister. Pastor Reid has died, but his influence still lives on, through me. Thanks, Pastor Reid.

Every contact leaves a message. The message may be good or bad. I am realizing that it is my responsibility to conduct myself so that when I leave your presence, I leave behind a good message or good feeling. It is my privilege to demonstrate this to every human being, whether in a personal meeting or on the telephone. After my next contact, I will want to know "What message did I leave behind?"

BE MY FRIEND

If this is you, then I am looking for you.
For my heart is crying out for you.
For there are a few things I desire more than a dear friend.

Who is the friend you are looking for?
Are you looking for a friend?
I imagine that there are many things occupying your life.
These things do bring you a degree of satisfaction and fulfilment.
But is that all? Could there be something missing?
And could that something be a friend?

There is no greater treasure than a good friend.
A friend is quick to point out your good points
And quick to hide away your failures

And lovingly walks you to where you grow.
A friend is one who knows you
And loves you in spite of you.

The greatest gift you can offer is the gift of true friendship.

True friendship is rooted in trust.

"A friend is as it were a second self" (Julius Caesar).

I am looking for a friend who will be there for me at all times and in all circumstances.

Several years ago, a little girl walked up to me and asked, "Will you be my friend?" I am sure I welcomed her thought and replied, "Yes." At that time, I did not really understand her question and what her needs were. But my answer was sufficient for her at that time. Today, I do not know where I would find that young lady, and if I found her, I wonder if she asked me the same question, "Will you be my friend?" if I would give the same answer, "Yes," and would I mean it and would she be satisfied with my answer and what would be my responsibility toward her?

It is my observation that many of us have several contacts who are courteous to us, who smile with us, and who seem to enjoy our company. This is great. We all need this type of relationship around us. But at the end of the day, many of us find ourselves wanting more than a smile and warm handshake. We, because of the challenges of life, want someone who has a heart like ours. Someone who understands and feels our heartbeats. Someone whose eyes are not frightened by our tears and whose cheeks are willing to absorb our tears and who will not run away from our nonsense behaviors, nor will tell others of our faults. We are looking for someone who will be there for us, always and under all circumstances.

Where are you, friend? Are you out there? Can I find you? Will you come to me and tell me that we are friends, forever friends?

And my world will be different, hopeful, and life will become the dream I have been having.

I know that there are a thousand places to go and things to do and when we are all done, there is little left to give anyone, not even ourselves. But how can we pass a broken heart on the side of the road, just because we have places to go?

THE DANCING DAYS

My days are not always good
Some days are bad
But I can face the bad days dancing
And with a good attitude

    All of us face each new day with expectations. We expect or hope for a good day. We hope that everything will go well; the kids will be happy and healthy, the cars and home equipment will work satisfactorily, everyone in the office will be nice and understand you, and the list can be extended. But sadly, these well-wishes fail us. For so often, things work out differently than what we had planned. And this brings heartaches and sadness.

    The other day, my car was acting up on me, and so I made an appointment to have it in the shop. I was on my way to the shop when the engine stopped. Fortunately it stopped where I could turn off the main road onto a parking lot. I tried everything to start it but without success. If only I could get it going, so I could get to the shop. But nothing worked. So what next? I called for a tow truck. No, I did not want to pay extra for towing service. Then waiting for the tow truck was another pain. But what else could I do?

    Sitting there waiting for the towing truck gave me some quiet time, and I found myself admiring the different vehicles as they drove by, the different makes and colors and people sitting behind the wheels. I found myself smiling. Then the towing truck arrived, and what a nice man the driver was. We were from the same city, and so conversation was easy and pleasant. We actually enjoyed each other during the short time we shared.

Why did my car stop when it was on its way to the shop? I did not know. And may never know. What I knew was I was off the road for a while, I spent some quiet time with passing vehicles and their drivers, and I met a very nice towing truck operator. And I got to the shop eventually and had my car fixed. The time my car was inoperative was my ***dancing*** moment. I had taken the time to be productive rather than worrying and fussing. Some would refer to this as dancing in the rain. Others see this as an opportunity for attitude change.

I have learned that regardless of the unplanned events in our lives, what really matters is our attitude. Are we able to see the positive in the negative? Are we able to dance in the rain? Are we able to make lemonade from lemon? Can we smile when we are disappointed? Can we understand and forgive when someone hurts us?

I do not always have good days. And when I have a bad day, I blend it with a good attitude and make a smoothie. And this provides me with energy for the day.

Please try these four approaches as you face each day:

1. Expectancy—Expect anything and everything. Things can change any moment.

2. Intentionality—At the beginning of the day, intentionally prepare yourself for the day. Tell yourself to be ready.

3. Sharing—Seek for the opportunity to reach out and share a good thought or deed with someone.

4. Thanksgiving—While there is consciousness, take the opportunity to give thanks for what did not happen and maybe for what happened.

Dear reader, may your days be ***dancing days.***

BEING NICE TO THE GROOM

We are never sure of what the day will bring us
We are never sure of what is around the corner
We are never sure of who is in the crowd
But this we can be sure of
Being nice always pays

It was my delight to travel to Charlotte, North Carolina, to officiate at my niece's wedding. The wedding was scheduled for Saturday morning. On that Thursday before, Lynn and I settled in the hotel, and I needed to return to the car for a few things. So I stepped out of our room and walked toward the elevator. While I was just a few yards from the elevator, a gentleman emerged from nowhere and walked toward me. He asked me if I knew where the elevator was, and I pointed him to it. And since I was heading there, we both walked along. As a conversation starter, I inquired if he was there for a wedding. He said yes. I further asked whose wedding it was. He replied that it was his. I was becoming more curious, so I asked if his name was Dixon and he said yes. "Steve Dixon?" I asked, and he replied, "Yes." We were becoming warmer by now, and so he asked me who I was.

"I am your new uncle." And soon we were hugging with excitement and wonder. Now, the wedding experience began here for me because I met the groom and the meeting was positive.

I am telling you about this incident to remind us that it is very important to be nice to everyone we meet. For we never know who it is we have just met. On another occasion, Lynn and I were vacationing in Jamaica. We stayed at a certain resort. In fact, we usually stayed at this resort and had met this nice staff member several times.

Looking back, we were always nice to her and she to us. Over a period of time, we became closer, and eventually Lynn and I became her parents and she was our Jamaican daughter. The relationship grew to such height that she asked me, her new daddy, to officiate at her wedding. I joyfully said yes. At this time of writing this story, I am planning to do her wedding in six weeks in Jamaica. How nice! I hope it is true for you as it is for me that it always pays to be nice because one never knows what will happen down the road. It pays to be nice to everyone we meet.

I prefer to say, "It is so nice to meet you again" and have pleasant memories because I was nice. It is a little distasteful to meet someone again after you were not nice. So why not be nice?

Dear reader, many of us meet people whom we do not know anything about. Our culture, which is becoming colder and freezing, has prepared us to become cold to people and mind our own business. And so it is easy to pass and ignore people. But I am appealing to you to appreciate that many people are open to our warmth and welcome. They will smile at us and even talk to us. Some will even open their hearts and tell us their story. This I know for sure. It happens daily with me.

I understand that some of us are timid to initiate the first words. But your timidity is not enough reason to deprive yourself of making a new friend, encouraging your own heart and brightening someone's day. If only you are courageous to reach out and be nice to someone, say hello, you will be planting a garden with flowers of all colors and kinds. And you will like it. Please try it. Be nice. Our world and culture need nice people. And I know you are nice. God bless you.

EXCITED THANKS

When the water is still
It is because there is nothing happening
When the wind is blowing or an object falls in
Then the water begins to move

  Everyone needs the water moving in his or her life. Everyone needs some excitement in his or her life which causes excitement, stimulation, or adrenaline activity. Where this is experienced, there tends to be thanksgiving, gratitude, joy, energy, positivity, and a search for opportunities to reach out and touch someone. This has happened to me repeatedly. On the other hand, when there is no activity in one's life, nothing to be grateful for, there tends to be a lackadaisical attitude, just taking life as it comes.
  It was my birthday, and I was at the church working in the garden among some rocks. At the end of the day, I could not find my car key. I looked everywhere among the rocks and bushes, everywhere I had been working that day. Someone suggested that I rent a metal detector, for this will find my key, but even with the metal detector, my key was not found. So eventually, I called home and Lynn rescued me. I could not wait for the next morning to return to the church, hoping to continue the search for my car key. So, here I am at the church, looking at the same places I looked the previous day. Then suddenly, down between the rocks, was a little silver shine, hardly visible to the eyes. My hands followed my eyes, and I could not believe what was sandwiched under the rocks. There was my car key, and what tumultuous joy and excitement flooded my being. Yes,

there was excitement, gratitude, thanksgiving, and adrenaline activity. I had a story to tell and reason to be joyful.

Another day, I left home with a Jumpdrive, intending to show to the printer some items contained on it. Arriving at the printer, I discovered there was no Jumpdrive in my pocket nor in my car. I knew I had it when I left home and when I had stopped by the church. Where could this Jumpdrive be, that which contained some important information? In fact, this book you are now reading was contained inside this Jumpdrive. So I frantically called home, but it was not there. I then hurried home and called the church, and it was not there. I called the printer hoping it was lying on the pavement where I was parked, but no, it was not there. What if it had fallen on the pavement at the church and a car crushed it?

So I hurried back to the church, looked on the pavement, inside the office, with no positive outcome. It was not there. Then I walked down the stairs where I had been, and behold, there was my Jumpdrive in a corner. Can you imagine the delight, gratitude which flooded me?

After I expressed thanksgiving for this finding, I hurriedly called home to spread the good news.

Not everyone every time will recover a lost item and may not be able to experience the adrenaline activity as I have been talking about. But, I hope everyone, even daily, will experience something which will ignite a measure of joy, thanksgiving, and gratitude. At least have this as a goal. You see, we all need this daily. Experiencing this will change our attitude toward life and rub off on others in our circle.

While I wish you will experience this, I also wish that you will join me in doing or saying something for someone which can cause a rush of joy, gratitude, and thanksgiving. For our world, communities, and homes can surely do with **excited thanks.**

No Stealing

When you have the floor, it's yours
I shall not take it from you
But wait for my turn

There is a commandment which says, "Thou shall not steal." Our world accepts the general principle of this commandment; stealing is wrong. And so we teach our kids from early days to respect this command or principle. Allow people to have and enjoy that which belongs to them. And those who disregard this might experience painful consequences.

In this section, I am introducing a ***stealing*** many of us are guilty of, yet without any serious consequence. I found myself grieving whenever it lifted its ugly head. We live with it. It happens all around us. It happens in all circles. Some people have fun committing this. Now, please journey with me to look at this ***stealing*** to see if you are guilty or innocent. Let me firstly confess, I have been guilty of this. This last time I was a victim, someone called me out and I was left embarrassed. Let us go there.

On this day I attended a meeting. At this meeting there was an invited guest presenter. Accompanying him were several other guests whom he introduced. They all belonged to the same organization and apparently worked together on some projects.

The invited guest speaker got into his presentation and was doing fine, according to my estimation. Everything was going fine until one of his guest attendees chose to intervene. She chose to add, explain, or contribute to what the guest presenter was saying. It did not occur to me that she added anything new or exciting, or what the presenter did not know. What was disturbing to me was she did not only add one or two sentences. No, she took over from the guest presenter. She behaved as if she knew everything about the subject, and she went on and on and on, while the guest speaker stood off to the side, it seemed. She stole the show. She took over the floor. And was she asked to do so? Surely not. Sadly for her, she did not know about this commandment, "Thou shall not steal." She did not know this. "Thou shall not steal the show nor the floor." It is one thing to throw in one word, one sentence, or two. This might be acceptable at times. But it is totally unacceptable to take over the presentation or discussion and go on and on and on. If the presenter wants our words, he or she will call for them.

It is my intention to remind us how we are to conduct ourselves when another person is speaking, whether it is a presentation or conversation. In a family situation when stealing occurs, we may hear an annoying statement like "Don't interrupt me," "You are interrupting me again." But in other situations like work or at meetings, we show restraints and courtesy. This is a good thing. Dear reader, let us help our people. Do not interrupt. Avoid showing how much we know. Avoid completing the speaker's sentence because in most cases, we really do not know what the speaker will say. If we have a valid contribution, wait for the appropriate time and ask permission to speak. To me, this looks like courtesy and respect. Then please remember, we do not always have to say anything, and if we do, wait for our turn. Don't steal the speaker's time nor thought. May I suggest this, ***Stealing*** can also be applied when we are with our family, coworkers, or friends.

Do I Have to Wait in Line?

The mail carrier may deliver a package
It may look good on the outside
You may think you know what's inside
But you may not know until you open it

    I stopped by my favorite Safeway store just to get a few things. What is interesting is I never know what is going to happen to me while there, for often there is something there for me, someone to meet, someone to encourage, or meeting a business partner. On this day, there was a lady behind me in the checkout line. As I usually do, I engaged her into a conversation and discovered that she was from out of town and only came to get a few items. We exchanged a few pleasantries, and as I was leaving, I suggested to the checker that she be extra nice to this lady for she was from out of town. The checker responded, "You mean by giving her a hug?" To this the shopper responded, "Yes, I love hugs." Hearing this, I stepped aside to see what would happen. Here it is. When the checker was through checking the few items of this out-of-town shopper, she stepped around from her machine, and met this lady and hugged her. Nice! Observing this, I too wanted to give this lady a hug, so I did. But this was not the end, for a shopper standing in line shouted, **"Do I have to wait in line?"** Can you see what is happening? The checker again gave away another hug, and so did I. Wow, what a morning!

    I am sure the out-of-town shopper left the store with a different feeling. The other lady who received her hug left with a story to tell. And now here I am telling you this story. And who knows how the other shoppers felt observing this?

If you were in that checkout line and observed the gift of free hugs, would you have desired one or not? I am aware that only some people appreciate hugs. Some shy away from hugs even from family and friends, more so from strangers. And this is fine. Then there are others who flourish on hugs, because it is said, "A hug a day keeps the doctor away." Personally, I love hugs and give hugs. And if you do not wish to have my hug, I respect you and will hold it to myself. And all of us are to be aware of the appropriateness of hugs.

But please allow me to broaden the hugs theme. You see, there are some who may resist having our hugs, but the same individuals may appreciate any of the following: a smile, hello, kind word, kind deed, humorous gesture, compliment, encouragement, or anything that will brighten the moment. On that morning when the hugs were exchanged, the checker said to me, "I love when you come by. You brighten my day."

Dear reader, people are occupied with bad news, bad situations, challenging issues, and are longing for light, cheerful, encouraging, caring moments. We are called upon to be there for these moments, and the opportunities may happen in the store, in the park, on the street, any place where there are people.

We never know who is waiting for a gift from us. We never know who is waiting for a moment they can appreciate.

A serviceman came to fix my sprinkler system. I shared with him the story of the hugs shared at Safeway. He liked it. Upon leaving, I thanked him for his work. He responded, "Do I have to wait in line for a hug?" And we exchanged hugs.

HAPPINESS

The voice of wisdom speaks
When we least expect
And says what shakes the mind
And there are times
When there is more beauty than meaning

    One early morning, Friday, August 19, 2016, I was awakened with a bundle of words. They were so clear as if written on a piece of parchment. But no, not on paper were they written, but on my mind. Never before had I experienced such strong and clear words. So I climbed out of bed, reached for a pen and paper, and began to write. The bundle of words were not quite clear, but beautiful. Here they are. See what you find in them.

Happiness

Happiness is finding me
And being content with whom I found

The pursuit of happiness
Then is
Walking intentionally
And looking expectantly
To find me

And settled happiness is
When I found me

I was just as was expected
in some ways
Different in other ways
Surprised in a few ways
And accepting in all ways

And then I realized
How much of a special gift I was
And I was happy
I found Happiness

Mangoes Are Nice

Niceness knows no barriers
Niceness is multilingual
Live it or speak it
For everybody understands it

Mangoes are one of my favorite fruits. So I stopped by the store to buy some. There was a large bin of all sizes. A lady joined me at the mango bin. Just to be sociable, I said to her ***"Mangoes are nice."*** It became obvious she did not speak English comfortably, so she gave me only a nod of the head and a smile.

I realized that the nod was all I would get from this lady, so I decided not to encourage any further conversation, but continued to make my mango choices. To my surprise, the lady came close to me by my side, and in her hands were two huge mangoes, maybe the biggest in the bin. She offered them to me with a smile.

Amazed, I gladly accepted them with a smile. And again, it became clear to me that niceness can be displayed without a verbal exercise. And again it became clear that when we talk to people, they may see that we are nice and will respond in kind.

A few minutes after this encounter, I saw the same lady in the store. Our eyes connected, and she smiled. This was because at the mango bin, I spoke to her.

I continue to experience that people want to be engaged. People want to know that we care. And when we reach out to them, they will reach out back to us.

Never Say Never

Brave men walk where they have never walked
Strong men lift weights bigger than themselves
Courageous men welcome the unknown
Successful men overcome the impossible

"Let's go on a cruise." I have heard this so many times. So many friends have invited Lynn and me to join them on a cruise. But my responses were always the same. "No," I would say. "I will never go on a cruise." For I knew that the least event I wanted was to be on a cruise. In fact, whenever I was invited or I just thought of it, I became annoyed. Now, please hear this. Lynn's nursing class was planning a cruise somewhere on the California-Mexico waters. This would be mostly couples. But I suggested that Lynn pair up with another nursing class friend so she would have a roommate. This worked and I was glad.

You see, my anticruise position was due to two fears: sleeping in a room under the water, and being in the middle of the ocean and seeing no land nor civilization for several days. No, no, this was not for me. "I would never go on a cruise," I would say.

After presenting a seminar in Southern California, I was invited to do another presentation, and it would be on a cruise. I said yes, and in ten weeks, I was on my first cruise from Long Beach, California, to Ensenada, Mexico. Oh yes, I enjoyed every moment. I loved it. I am ready for my next cruise.

Maybe I shall stay away from saying, "I will never." Maybe I will be fair to myself and give myself a chance and be open to an adventure. The ones who adventure are challenged to greater and bigger vistas.

Start a Conversation

*Don't be afraid to start a conversation.
Just start it. It may go nowhere, but you will
never know unless you started it.*

At the store, I stood in the checkout line. Immediately behind me was a lady with about six kids, ranging from ages three to seven. Admiring the kids, I asked the lady if the children were hers, to which she replied that some were and the others were not, but adopted.

I turned to the kids to engage them in conversation. And they were not at all shy but fired right back at me. One kid volunteered that he had lost a tooth. And suddenly, the topic of the conversation was about missing teeth. It seemed that each one had a story about his missing tooth. It was a lively conversation.

By now it was time to check out, and soon I was leaving. So I said goodbye to the kids. Like a choir, they, all with a high volume and enthusiasm, responded, "Goodbye, goodbye," enough to fill that corner of the store with sunshine. Other shoppers were caught up in the spirit, and all looked to see what was happening. Whatever it was, it was because I simply **started a conversation.**

Next time you see some kids, why not **start a conversation?** You might be surprised at the result.

STAY ON TOP

Let no one take your gold
This might be all you will get

Each new day brings challenges
Each challenge brings opportunities
Each opportunity is a call for us to decide;
Which way we will go
What are we going to do
Whatever you do, please take the following
into consideration

When you are up, stay up
When you are down, climb up and don't come down
It is easier to fall than to climb
It is easier to fall from joy than to build joy
Don't allow anyone to take your joy
Don't allow anyone to *take your gold*
It is your purse with all your change
Follow no one's footsteps
unless they are leading you upward

And while you are heading upward
Why not take someone along with you?

Exceptional People

Push yourself to become the very best you can be
Never settle for anything less
Compete with yourself, until you are satisfied
That you are ahead of yourself

We have all seen the athlete, beating his/her body until the intended goal is reached. We have seen the concert pianist spending hours upon hours on the piano, hoping to achieve the intended goal. And usually, they do. Why? Because they disciplined themselves to strive, push, excel, to become the ***exceptional people***.

I am wondering, have you ever thought of becoming an exceptional person, friend, boss, employee, Christian, Muslim, spouse, parent, child, citizen, _____ _____?

I hope you have. And I hope you still share that ideal. I realize that I am retired from full-time pastoring, but I am still on board motivating people to climb their mountains, to climb to the top. I am encouraging you to become or strive to become, or continue to strive to become that ***exceptional person***, in the field of your choice. Whatever you set out to do, give it your all.

We were created to be that ***exceptional person.*** It is within our reach. Let us bring delight to ourselves, because we are excelling to be the best we can be.

Just a Few Moments

*It takes **just a few moments** to create a good deed,
which makes memories that may last forever.
And everyone has these **few moments**.*

George and I worked together for years at the church's annual camp meetings in Gladstone, Oregon. Sadly, George had a stroke, which severely limited his activities and was no longer able to work at camp meetings, an event which meant the world to him. Knowing this, it took me just a **few moments** to arrange for George to be at the 2015 camp meeting, uniformed in his red shirt, badge, and name tag, just as if he was a worker. He was assisted onto a golf cart and given a tour of the camp grounds, taken to the places where he would have gone in former years. Then after the tour and meeting several individuals, we positioned him at the main plaza, where the crowd of people was stationed. There, sitting in his special chair, brought by his wife, Renee, George had the joy of meeting many of his friends. Hearts were touched, and tears trickled. George left for home after being there for a few hours, for he was tired. But I knew he left with memories which will last forever.

Stay in Line

It is better to stand in line than to change lines.

—*Anonymous*

Many of us have been to the grocery store and sometimes in a little hurry and hope to get into the shortest line. So we look around and are unsure which is the faster line, number 3 or number 5. Finally we decide that number 5 will be the faster, so we change lines from number 3 to number 5. Then frustratingly, we stand in line just to see the person in the colorful shirt, who was in line number 3, walk by pushing her cart. And here we are still in line, two customers back, waiting for a price check.

Sometimes the same thing happens in traffic to those of us who want to get ahead faster. The lane we thought would go faster becomes the slower lane.

There are times in life when it is better to stay with: Your old plan, your old friend, your old house, your old car, your old idea, or just **stay in line.**

There are times when we are placed in line number 3 to meet the person who comes behind us, or to place us on the street at the right time.

Planting Roses

Let her plant her roses.
For while she is in her garden planting, this
might be the only happiness she will get.

Georgia and Margie were having a happy conversation. They were sharing their life's journey. Georgia told the story of the time she was stopped by a police officer for speeding. While the officer was checking her papers, she spent the time praying that he would show her mercy. So the officer returned to her window with her papers and gave her a lecture and warning instead of a ticket. She drove away, happy, praising God and singing, for God had answered her prayer. She received mercy instead of a ticket of one hundred dollars or more.

As Georgia recalled and told this story, she became excited, for what God and the police officer did for her was good news.

In response to her story and excitement, Margie came back and said, "I wouldn't be too excited about this. I think the officer just had a bad day and didn't know what to do with you. That sometimes happen to them for that happened to me once."

This is taking the wind away from one's sail.
This is taking the joy out of one's life.
This is taking away the **roses** one is planting.
Let people plant their **roses**.

Love Left on My Car

Sometimes, it is the little things that matter.
And they go farther than the giver intended.

I walked to my car at the end of church
There sat on my front window a daffodil
And on the rear window was a camellia
They sparkled in the brightness of the sun
They were beautiful to behold
But more than beauty was what they said
"Ewart, you are loved"
At home they paraded from a vase
And each time I walk by they sang to me
"Ewart, you are loved"
One morning as I walked by I said
"Good morning, love"

The next morning as I walked out of the house
I looked at them and said
"Goodbye, love"

I gave thanks to the heart and hands
That planted a little love beside me
And for me

My Day

Everyone has a day
A day when the heart is troubled
A day in need of comfort
A day to receive encouragement
A day to give encouragement

One ***day***, I received an e-mail. On that ***day***, my heart needed that e-mail. It came at the right time. After reading and rereading it, I connected with the sender, thanked him, and got his permission to share it with you. Here it is.

> *Ewart, I haven't seen you around lately and I have missed your smiling and friendly face! I just wanted to make sure you're doing OK, my brother.*
>
> *You do such a great job of seeking out others. I want you to know that others seek you, too!*
>
> *I trust you're just having a great time, as usual, but know that I was thinking about you and am hoping everything is well!*
>
> *Take care,*
> *Jason*

That was ***my day***. And to you, dear reader, may your ***day*** come to receive a note like this. May your ***day*** come to send a note like this. For we all need a ***day*** like this.

People and Projects

*Most times we can reschedule our projects.
But most times, we should never reschedule people.
For there might be only one chance to hear them.*

One of the things I do is gardening at my church. I enjoy keeping the grounds clean and attractive. Because of the many other projects occupying my time, I had neglected the grounds for a few weeks. It was very obvious that fall cleaning needed to be done, so I scheduled myself to be there.

So I gathered my tools and wheelbarrow and moved into position to work. Just then, one of our neighbors saw me and walked toward me. Now what? The day was swiftly running away, and I had not yet eaten that day, so I must hurriedly get the work done and be gone. But here comes my neighbor to visit as we had done several times before.

Then in that moment, my heart told me that ***people*** were more important than ***projects.*** Therefore, I parked my wheelbarrow and joyfully walked over to meet my neighbor, and we had a long happy visit. At the end of our time, we both agreed that our time together was very beneficial. I left feeling very good, even with less ***projects*** done. But what was more important was **people**. *People* are more important than ***projects.***

God's Time Clock

*When your day is placed in God's hands, you
are setting yourself up for a miracle.*

It has been my practice to begin my day with placing my plans in God's care. This is when I ask Him to direct all my activities for that day. I am going to tell you the story of how precisely God directed my plans one Tuesday.

There were several things on my agenda for that day. Only two of them were specifically assigned by time. I had to be there on time. The others were totally up to me, and I had no specific reasons to be at the post office, the dentist, or the bank at a certain time. Somehow, after several stops, I ended up at the bank just to say hello to the staff.

At the bank, I usually have one certain teller assist me. This time I went to another teller to make a social call, since my teller was busy. I was about to leave and just say a quick hello to my teller, since she had just answered a telephone call. I went to shake her hand, and she held on to my hand. She said, *"Please don't leave."* As I stood, her tears began to fall in rapid succession as her countenance changed to distress. She hanged up the phone, and from her shaking lips, she told the story of her dad's medical condition. It was not good. But she thanked me for coming at the precise time when she needed me. This was **God's timing.**

THANKS BUT NO THANKS

*You can make my day
But I won't let you ruin my day.*

—Carol Fisher

Carol is a friend of mine. We worshipped together for several years. In her life's journey, she is constantly interacting with people and experiences the swing of people's emotions and behaviors. In one of our exchanges of experiences, she shared these two lines with me. They are nice and short, but dynamic. Wherever I use these lines, people stop and ponder before saying a word.

Why not? Many of us begin our day with great intentions to live happily and change the world. Then comes someone, and by what is said or done, the atmosphere of the moment changes. And all our dreams for that moment or day shatter. Not a good idea. The question is did that person shatter our dreams? Or did we allow our dreams to be shattered? I love what Carol said to me, *"You can make my day, but I won't let you ruin my day."*

I added this to Carol's Lines: "I will not allow anyone, anything, to take my joy. For it is a gift to keep, to share, and not to be taken."

The next time someone offers you pleasure, say, ***"Thanks."*** If you are offered pain, say, ***"No thanks."***

Someone

Some days, what I long for most is just someone.

- *Someone to care*
- *Someone to be me*
- *Someone to carry me*
- *Someone to lift me up*
- *Someone to accept me*
- *Someone to hold my heart*
- *Someone to sit in my chair*
- *Someone to share my tears*
- *Someone to cheer at my wins*
- *Someone to sorrow at my losses*
- *Someone to understand my fears*
- *Someone to understand my tears*

Just someone.

Disappointment

I don't like disappointment
But if it makes me better
Then I guess it's all right

No one likes disappointment
It throws us off
It spoils our plans
We have to start all over

And yet, sometime
It is disappointment that drives
us to a new plan
that turns out better than we had thought

And had we known from the beginning
We would have started here

Thanks, disappointment
You are a friend
Not a foe

Knowing Who I Am

*Life is not only about what you can offer the
world or what the world can offer you.
It's mostly about being totally honest and present with yourself,
knowing who you are and where you want to go.*

  I began my early years in Jamaica and did well with the resources available to me. Looking back, I can see where I was strong and where I was weak. Fortunately, I was able to overcome my weaknesses. But how much different my life could have been if I were invited to look at me objectively and see who I truly was, accept who I was, celebrate the positives, and retrain the negative or walk away from the negative.

  It took me many years to be able to accept who I really am and where I want to go in life, and I am so much more comfortable with myself. I even like me. Why? Because I know that I am a special creation with a unique purpose. There is no one quite like me. As is said, when God was finished making me, He threw away the copy. Wow!

  We collect insights and grow when we observe the upward trends of others. But never to covet another person's life. We are to be and celebrate who we were created to be. Someone might be watching you and want to grow from your genuine walk of life.

THE SECOND ANGEL

*Listen to someone's heart.
For the same heart might be listening to yours.*

It was at a Saturday evening social where I met Carol. Our casual conversation soon was translated to a higher level. We began to talk about relationships between people. She talked to me about a meeting between her and a lady whom she had not seen for about fifteen years. What was touching about this meeting was this lady talked about her life story, even though they had not connected for many years.

I remarked to Carol that the lady's need was to talk to someone and that she represented many others who just wanted someone to talk to. I complimented Carol for listening to the lady and told her she was an angel. Carol came right back and said, "That lady was an angel." From this response, I realized that the heart-pouring lady did something for Carol, the listener. I did not question what really happened between them. I was only caught up with the transaction between them. For a while I thought Carol was an angel for listening; now Carol saw this lady as **the second angel.**

The next time someone wants to pour out to you a hurting heart, please take time to listen. While you might be an angel for listening, the other person might be **the second angel.**

Glendora Barber

If you want to get a jump on life, do what no one has ever done.

    Lynn and I were vacationing in the city of Glendora, California. I was scheduled to speak at a church that weekend. Looking clean and proper were important to me, which included a fresh hair look. So that Friday, before the Saturday when I would speak, I looked for a barber to touch up my hair. I found one. And she was amazing.

    She did a super job touching up my hair, that is sharpening the lines. But she did more. She trimmed my eyebrows and trimmed hairs from my ears. This was impressive, because no barber had ever done this in my lifetime. I was so touched and pleased that I secured her name and business telephone number. I told her how pleased I was and assured her that whenever I was visiting Glendora, I would return to have her do my hair.

    Why would I return? Because she did for me what no one else had ever done. Reflecting on this, I realized that one can **get a jump on life**, or be on the cutting edge when he or she stretches and goes beyond the ordinary, does what no one has ever done.

    Yes, it is true, the next time I am in Glendora, California, I will be going for a hair touch-up and hope to get that same barber.

THE TRAFFIC STOP THAT SHOCKED

Everyone needs a breath of fresh air
To vitalize one's life for the day
It may come to you from someone
Or you may choose to give it to someone

Lynn and I had been in Jamaica for my cousin's funeral service and were driving in a rental car to the airport to fly home. We were cruising along talking about our delightful Jamaica experiences. The weather was charming, and so were the sceneries. I was driving according to the speed limit, I thought.

Then on the side of the road was a white-marked car and two nicely dressed uniformed men. One stepped toward me and waved at me, and I understood that he meant for me to stop. Yes, I stopped, and many thoughts were running through my mind. The police officer asked for the documents for the car and my driver's license. Then he said, "The reason that I stopped you is because you're exceeding beyond the speed limit."

I said, "Officer, I am sorry. Speeding is not my style."

"I know," he replied. "And where are you going?"

"I am going back home to Oregon."

He returned my papers and said, "Have a good trip."

"Thanks, Officer," I replied.

Then I looked at him and maybe blew his mind when I said this: "Officer, I just want to tell you thanks for what you do here in Jamaica. I know that you are not always appreciated, and while many are sleeping, you are up keeping them safe and sometimes your life is a lonely life. Sir, I appreciate you and thanks." I reached out and shook his hand, and he smiled as we said goodbye. I sensed that this moment to him was like a breath of fresh air. I was glad I had the courage to offer this. Why not try something like this someday?

First Class

Treat a person with dignity.
And that person will act with dignity.
Treat a person with despair.
That person will tend to act underclass.

If you have ever traveled by plane and found yourself in first class, then you know what I am about to share. If you have never been in first class, then allow me to serve you just a taste.

Lynn and I were returning from Jamaica and found ourselves in first class. This was not our first time, but this time it seemed especially impactful. As first class passengers, we were among the first ones who boarded; the first ones to be served drinks; the only ones who were served real lunch, unless you purchased one; given warm towels to wash or freshen up; cloth covering for our trays, cloth napkins; your personal coats or jackets taken and stored and seemingly anything to add comfort. I became conscious of how I should behave. My behavior should be royal, because I was treated royally.

Have you ever felt like you were a first class person? Has someone ever seen the values and virtues in you and walked alongside you, and at the end of the journey, you felt like you were in first class or was a first class person?

The other question I am asking is have you made someone feel first class?

On this journey of life, please look for opportunities to make someone first class. There are so many who will appreciate it.

LIVING THE GOOD LIFE

Life is about experiencing and appreciating the little things
Those things which will impact your life
And the lives of those around you

Ten Trees to be planted
In the garden of
The good Life

Have a plan
Have a faith
Have a friend
Have resources
Be in good health
Give yourself away
Have a positive attitude
Wear a smile on your face
Connect with a youth/child
Do a good deed for someone

Munchies for Life

Remember, the way you live will impact you and your community. So it is imperative that you live the best you can.

Leave footprints behind
Stretch beyond yourself
Believe in yourself
Help one in need
Meet new people
Be inspirational
Be encouraging
Keep the cool
Like yourself
Be positive
Have fun
Keep fit
Laugh
Live

Rejected and Resurrected

*If you see it, feel it, and believe it
Then why not say it?*

Someone gave me a sweater for Christmas. It was a gray one. Now, if I had gone to the store to shop for a sweater, it is not likely that you would see me walking from the store with a gray sweater or grey anything. You see, my favorite colors are blue, red, burgundy, pink, purple, and lavender. Surely not gray. So what did I do with the gray sweater? Right, I carefully stored it away.

One day, as I was looking through my things, I ran across this gray sweater and decided to take a chance and wore it. Why did I do this? That day, about three individuals enthusiastically commented on how great I looked and how the gray sweater and my black slacks were the in thing. Wow! Based upon those comments, the next day, I again wore the same combination. Again someone else commented. Wow! Wow!

Since then, this combination has become my frequent favorite dress code, gray and black. Why? Because someone **saw it, felt it, believed it, and said it** to me. Thanks to you who took time to tell me. Even my gray sweater is thankful to you.

The next time you **see it, feel it, and believe it, why not say it?** It might make a big difference. You might give someone the motivation to do what he or she would not have done.

From Me to You

The time is right to make the switch
From me to you

Based upon the music I listen to and the thoughts I hear expressed on the radio or television, I heard myself saying at the beginning of the day, "Lord, You are going to do something special for **me** today." Looking back into my experience, I have been saying this for some time. But recently, I examined what I have been saying, though a noble statement, and determined that, that statement was very self-serving. It was all about **me**.

So I have adjusted that statement to become more outreaching and "otherly." Thus it reads, "Lord, You are going to do something special for someone today, **you** through **me**."

I am learning that when life is all about **me**, my world is dark and cloudy. On the other hand, when I make life all about **you**, the world seems lighter and clearer. I am distracted from selfishness and attracted to the consciousness of otherness.

In this fast lane world, when most of us want to be in the overpass lane, which means speeding past others, I am begging us to slow down and help the ones we are passing. Wherever we are attempting to reach, please remember that the other persons desire to reach there also. What if the both of us could reach the same time together?

Please, let us remember, the world is not just for **me**. It's for **you** also. It's for us. I will direct the emphasis ***from me to you.***

FLOWERS AND DRIED LEAVES

While some see the brokenness
Others see the beauty

It was springtime and garden cleaning time. And since it was a nice day, I decided to spend some time in the garden, cleaning and pulling weeds. When I stepped outside, the first thing that caught my attention was some ugly dried leaves hanging from a bed of Helleborus plants (an evergreen perennial flowering plant, grows about one foot off the ground, remains green all year, and produces white or red flowers). So I gathered my tools and immediately began to cut and remove the ugly dried leaves.

Just then, Lynn, my wife, walked outside and noticed what I was about to do. The first words from her lips were amazingly shocking, "Aren't the flowers beautiful?" It was shocking to me to realize that until Lynn spoke about the beauty of the flowers, I had not seen the flowers nor their beauty. Then I paused to look and what beauty they radiated. Realizing what had just happened to me, I asked myself, "Ewart, why didn't you see the flowers, but only the dried leaves, even though they were so close together?"

In real life, so many times we see only the ugly dried leaves, not the flowers. And about people, often, we see only their faults and not their good deeds. Flowers are more beautiful than dried leaves. Good deeds are worth more than faults. Let us learn to see the beautiful flowers and the good things people do.

BURGER KING WORKER

If you are not smiling and not laughing, then you are not living.

—*Burger King Worker*

I stopped by Maps Credit Union and in conversation with one of the workers, the short story that is about to knock you over was shared with me. So relax and hear it.

Maricela said she needed something to eat, and for some reason she was not happy that day. She was in a bad mood. So she drove to Burger King restaurant (Keizer Station), and at the menu board she placed her order. Through the intercom came the happy voice of a young man, and she liked it. At the window, as she paid for her order, she noted the young teenager, maybe sixteen, was smiling and happy. She said to him, "You are super happy today." And to this the young man replied, "If you are not smiling and not laughing, then you are not living." Wow!

To this Maricela replied to the young man, "There needs to be more people like you in this world." True!

I was fully absorbed in this story, and as Maricela continued to comment on her experience, she then said, "This sixteen-year-old just slapped me back into my place."

Thanks, Maricela, for the story, and thanks to you, sixteen-year-old young Burger King worker. I may never meet you, but your message has affected me and will travel into many lives here and all over the world. Dear reader, remember to smile and be happy.

A Helping Hand

Give me life
That I might give life
To a struggling life

Today, a springlike day, I was out in the garden pulling weeds and pruning our climbing roses trailing the fence. There tangled in the roses was one grapevine struggling for life. Because I like grapes and had harvested grapes from that cluster each year, I carefully protected that struggling vine. I placed it where I would not cut it, but several times, it found itself in my grip, and each time, I remembered to save it, give it a chance to live and grow, for soon it might produce grapes.

I am reminded that the challenge for every person, every day, is to realize that he or she has a responsibility to affect a life for the better. We are here to live and help others live. We are here to help lift others to greater heights. We are here to walk with those who are trying to walk, are limping, and can hardly make it.

You see, at the end of the journey, the real praise will not be for only those who made it, but more for those who helped someone to make it or brought someone along.

Today, you may encounter someone on life's journey struggling. Why not take a moment to offer ***a helping hand***?

Fire and Grass

It is hard to start a fire where there is no grass.
Fire needs substance to feed on, to give it energy.

We all have heard of grass fires. This refers to a section of land of grass which is consumed by fire. Grass fires are fast and furious, and for this reason, the fire control people will put in place a controlled fire. This means, controlling the fire as it consumes the grass. The path of the fire is determined. And if a greater fire comes, it will be ineffective, because there is nothing to burn. This is important. There is nothing to burn. Fire has to have substance to live.

In our daily lives, there are times when a fire comes to consume us to burn us down. But often this fire can be effective only if there are substances in us to feed it, to give it energy. To counter this fire, we must remove or eliminate fire-feeding substances.

If there are substances in our homes which encourage certain undesirable behaviors, we are better off with them gone. If there are individuals around us who encourage certain undesirable behaviors, we are better off when they are less frequent. If certain conversations tend to lead to an undesirable outcome, then such maybe should be deleted from our pages. If every time certain things are said, we become upset, vocal, and uncontrolled, then we should try saying nothing and be calm. Say nothing, and maybe nothing will be said in return. For fire needs grass to glow.

A Word a Day

A word a day
Keeps the doctor away

Over the years, I have heard the sayings:
"An apple a day keeps the doctor away."
"A banana a day keeps the doctor away."
"An avocado a day keeps the doctor away."
In these recent days, as I live among humanity and care-connect with them, I have discovered that another line can very definitely be added:
"A word a day, keeps the doctor away."
So each day, let us live one of these words, and notice how it will change someone's life.

Today, I choose:
    To be **nice**
    To be **kind**
    To **involve**
    To **listen**
    To **clarify**
    To **esteem**
    To be **positive**
    To be **cheerful**
    To **encourage**
    To give **respect**
    To show **interest**
    Live a word and lift a life.

A Line a Day

*A line a day
Keeps the doctor away*

Try saying a ***line a day*** and see what happens. We say so much, and often nothing happens. Now, try these, please.

Today, I choose to say:

*I love you.
I am sorry.
I thank you.
I appreciate you.
What can I do for you?
I will do anything for you.
I have always wanted to do something nice for you.
I will always treasure your nice, warm thoughts.
I enjoy being in your presence.
Please call me. I will be waiting.*

Say a line and save a life.

Sadness to Joys

When the darkness sets in, then it is time to see the stars.
When the electricity goes out, then it is time to enjoy the candlelights.

We arrived in Jamaica where we would be for ten days. When we arrived at the resort, we learned that our room was not ready. This was not good news, for we were tired. But since we had relatives living close, we went to visit them, hoping that our room would be ready when we returned. But again, it was not. So another room was offered to us, and when we walked in, we were miserably disappointed and returned to the lobby. In the lobby, I met one of the directors who understood our dilemma and placed us in a luxury room with its own personal pool. Wow! This turned out pretty good. Joyous, wouldn't you say?

On another occasion, Lynn and I were returning from Jamaica, flying from Montego Bay to Atlanta, Georgia, and then on to Portland, Oregon. We missed our connecting flight from Atlanta to Portland and had to overnight in Atlanta. I was disappointed, since I had an important meeting the next day in Portland. However, Delta Airlines rebooked us for the first flight the next day and upgraded us to first class. Not too bad? Not at all.

Sometimes, when things seem bad, maybe that is the birth of goodness and joys. Sometimes, that which seems sad will soon turn to joys. And missing our connecting flight to Portland could have meant that we were not to be in Portland that night. Who knows? I am learning to give thanks for all things.

SNACK PACKS

Snack Packs

Is a compilation of gems from my reservoir
and a few from other sources.
They are intended to be motivational and inspirational.
They may push you, lead you, or just energize your mind.
As I have enjoyed creating these, may you
also enjoy having them beside you.

Nothing can stop a positive person
Nothing you do can help a negative person.

Some people tell you how they feel
Others show you
While the others neither show nor tell.

The language of friendship is not all words
But also presence.

There is no greater treasure than a good friend.

"A friend is as it were a second self" (Julius Caesar).

A friend is quick to point out your good points
And quick to hide away your failures.

A friend is one who knows you
And loves you in spite of you.

The greatest gift you can offer
Is the gift of true friendship.

Life is a gift. Every day is a privilege.

Make a big deal out of the little things.

Where bitterness resides
Happiness avoids
And keeps walking.

"Be kind for everyone you meet is fighting a battle" (John Watson).

"Feeling gratitude and not expressing it,
Is like wrapping a present and not giving
it" (William Arthur Ward).
In the middle of every difficulty
Lies an opportunity.

"You can make my day,
But I won't let you ruin my day" (Carol Fisher).

Today is a gift. Take it and wear it.

If I can give you just one advice for your journey
It is "be NICE."

Life is not only about what you can offer the world or what the world can offer you. It's mostly about being totally present with yourself knowing who you are, where you want to go, and what you want to do for someone, then doing it.

Today's trouble doesn't empty tomorrow of its pains
But only empties today of its joys.

At the dawn of day
Package some love for the Creator
Appreciation for yourself
And a gift for a friend.

When you are up, stay up
When you are down, climb up and don't come down
It is easier to fall than to climb
It is easier to fall from joy than to build joy

Don't allow anyone to take your joy
It is your purse with all your change

"When you know your value you don't beg people to like you.
Everyone can't afford the luxury of having
your friendship" (Anonymous).
Learn everything
Give some things
Listen much
Talk little
Don't show your entire picture album

When a person calls, it's for information.
When a friend calls, it's for connection.

A friend gives you;
His heart
His presence
Memories so pleasant
A piece of himself
A desire to keep him
And a longing for him

Don't say the obvious, especially when it leans to the negative.

Those who insist on vindication do need
a vacation for self-inspection.

Here is what I am thinking. But do you want
to know even if it's not gossip?

If meeting you were like a refreshing meal,
What would you want me to serve you,?
Hug, smile, touch, short story, listening? What else?

When after you have left one's presence
And it is wished that you would come back soon,
Then you know that you have been socially relevant.

I spent the whole day in misery and wished
someone had given me a minute of joy

What can I say
What can I do
What can I be
That will make a difference
For someone?

I think it
I meditate on it
I write it
I desire to do it
I pray about it
Yet it is hard to do it
Lord, have mercy on me

The goal of humanity is
To worship the Creator
Grow within the circle of a family
Care-connect with other human beings
And so live to make this world a better place

Do not wait for life
It is here
Just live it

Stretch beyond yourself
Believe in yourself
Help one in need
Meet new people
Be inspirational
Be encouraging
Keep the cool
Like yourself

Be positive
Have fun
Be fun
Keep fit
Laugh

I was so busy taking care of me that I didn't see the pain in your face, nor the tears in your eyes, and the heart that cared for me.

Now that you are here with me, what can I say or do
that will make you feel warm and significant?
What others say or do may make me feel significant, but
more important is what I know and feel about myself.

If I gave you everything I had, all I would want in return is nothing.

Gratitude and attitude make altitude.

An attitude of gratitude brings altitude.

If you want to reach an altitude, walk with a healthy attitude.

"May your complaints be few and expressions of your gratitude be compounded" (Maynard Hanna).

Watch your humor.
To someone else, it may be a tumor.

Give someone your best.
On this day, it might be all she gets.

Thanks, disappointment.
You are a friend, not a foe.

Mistakes in life make better pathways.

Even when I make a wrong turn, I can always find a turnaround.

When we part ways
Whether for today or by death
What do you want me to remember about you?
What about you may I bottle and take with me?

"Smooth seas do not make great sailors" (African saying).

See the fruits in your garden,
Not the fallen leaves,
Unless they are for decoration.
See the smiles and joys in your life,
Not the tears and terrors,
Uunless they are for edification.

Do you have a friend you can just walk to and spill your guts?
Where in the world are they these days?

My life may be a struggle.
But every morning I am awake,
I give God thanks for I have life.

The minute of your time you give someone
Could change that life for a lifetime.

Multilingualism is
Understanding the different ways
Your friend tells you she cares
And enjoys being in your presence.

When was the last time
You put away the business of the moment
To watch a butterfly dance from leaf to leaf?

A morning prayer;
Lord, today I want to love You.
And then I want to love someone
In such a way that will entice that someone
To love You and the world around."

Has your heart ever skipped a beat
Because you saw someone
Grow right before your very eyes?
If not, could it be you were looking
in the wrong direction?

"You are an angel."
Has anyone ever said this to you?
If yes, why, what was intended?

Just be nice
It's not complicated

Here is a bottle for holding treasures
Bottle a treasure from me and take it with you
Position it where it can be seen
Remove the cover and release me
That I may be with you
I am better
Outside the bottle

I have not lived
Until my life has given life to someone

It is a beautiful story when you;
Tell me how much you care
And how far you would go
To bring comfort and happiness
And how significant I am

And how you have brought yourself to me
Please tell me that story again and again

It is important to know who I am
It is equally important;
What others know about me
By what I say and what they see
For who I am is only important
When it connects with others
And makes a difference

People will remember you for what you did
Not so much what you thought

Where nothing is planted
Nothing grows
Except weeds

Gratitude kills negative germs
And builds mental health

Give someone a reason to smile
And you would have recreated his world

Though you have hurt me
And have not been speaking to me
And we are not buddies
Yet I will care
And bring you a cold drink
On a hot day

When you give a half story
You get a half answer
When you give a full story

You deserve a full answer

"Spot the sprout"
Look for the little things
Sometimes they are right in your face

Put your eggs into the nest
Where it will be nurtured
And bring forth baby birds

Too much vexation
Is an invitation
To a vacation
For rejuvenation

God loves me
More than words can say
God loves me
Bigger than all my friends combined
God loves me
Longer than all the rivers joined together
God loves me
So much, I feel like a honeybee
In a garden of flowers

A friend is like a sweet-smelling cologne
That I spray on me
That refreshes my air
That I carry for memories
That tells others
Something sweet is around

Sometimes
It is time to just play
And not plan

Care enough to want to know
How I am feeling

Everything you hear
Is an opportunity to exercise
Your screening ability

The true value of life is measured by how many faces you lit
How many people are walking around saying,
"You light up my life"?

To Be a PIE
Be Positive
Inspire
Encourage

If you expect it
You may never get it
If you don't expect it
You may get it
Whether you get it or not
Be strong and live above it

If you don't have a goal
It's because you are on the wrong team
And you are not kicking the right direction

It is the broken twigs
That the robin takes
To make a bed for creating life

If today were your last day to live
Where would you live it?
With whom would you live it?
What would your last words be?

Why?

It's not about how well we work together
It's about how well we feel working together
It's not how well we get along
It's how important each one feels

Be intentional to do
The unnatural

While travelling on the sea of life
And we run out of gas
And the engine quits
Just put up the sails
And God will send the wind

Turn something small to something memorable

Don't advertise what you cannot produce
Stock your shelves first
People are tired of staring at empty shelves

Today, I am giving you my friendship
In times like these friendship is beautiful
I am giving you my heart
And as you process life's challenges
Just know that my friendship
Closes in beside you
I am singing for you
I am planting flowers for you
I am waving my arms
In order to create a still breeze around you
I am spreading my wings
In order to form sheltering clouds over you
And I am spreading my coat for you to step on

To keep the shine on your shoes
Now look ahead, and there is the sunrise
Look behind, there is the moon
And in the shadow is a little quiet smile
From me to you

People want to walk beside lifters
But walk away from loaders

A daily prayer:
Lord, make me a giving tree
Plant me at an intersection
Where people of all kinds walk
And give me the eyes to see them
And the heart to know what they are crying for
That I may offer them a cup of water or a candy

Go for the moon
If you don't quite get there
You would have seen more than millions

Speak your stuff
One can't read your mind

See the visible
See also the possible

Your life is a coat of many colors
It's beautiful
Wear it
Share it
Turbulence is
Two people on a journey
But only one knows the way

Leave a good feeling behind
People will hold it until you return
They will remind you of it
And will want more

Sometimes the best gift I can give to you
Is just to listen to you

When I don't know what to say nor do
I will just cuddle beside you

It is more a desirable delight
To be in a room with few friends
Than being in that same place
With plenty people

One close friend
Is worth more than
One hundred individuals

People come in a cruise ship
Friends come in a Mini Cooper

When you can't see around the bend
Don't imagine what's there
Just drive carefully

When people talk to people
There is less silence, less pain
And more cheerful moments

Life's difficulties are here
To make us better
Not bitter

Connections are not accidents
But opportunities
What you do with them is what matters
It is not the length of the connection
That matters
It is the utilization of the time allowed

It is the fallen rain
That brings life to the ground

"When everything seems to be going against you, remember that the airplane takes off against the wind, not with it" (Henry Ford).

"If God brings you to it, He will bring
you through it" (Anonymous).

"Laughter is an instant vacation" (Anonymous).

Don't steal another person's punch line.
He might have worked hard for it.

"If you want to lift yourself up, lift up someone
else" (Booker T. Washington).

Some people have the ability to drive you crazy
yet do not know how to make you happy.

The shine from the sun
Is not only in the clouds
It's also in me

If my life is a mirror
What do people see?

Take time to look, play, and smile with a baby
Or just watch a butterfly dance from petal to petal

No one likes disappointment
It throws us off
It spoils our plans
We have to start all over
And yet, sometimes
It is disappointment that drives
Us to a new plan
That turns out better than we had thought

Allow someone to open his mind to you
And you might be giving him a gold mine

Give away your heart
And you may find at your door
A whole body waiting for you

I will not allow anyone, anything
To take my joy
For it is a gift
To keep
To share
And not to be taken

Life is a decision
An opportunity
Not a chance

If you want to gain altitude in life
Build an elevator from gratitude
It is good to give your means
It is better to give your wisdom
It is best to give your heart

The little things
To the little people
Are big things

When I plan to build a behavior
I will plan to build a good behavior
For too often we spend a lot of time
Planning that which hurts
And less time planning that which heals
When a monkey is on my back
I can plan how to throw it to the ground
Or plan how to give it a smooth ride

There are lots of delivery trucks and vans
All over town
And when I see them,
I am reminded to ask myself,
"What am I delivering today?"
And I pray this prayer:
"Lord, load on my truck today
Boxes of joy, hope, smiles, kindness
And encouragement."

When you have something good to offer
You don't have to beg anyone to come
For a piece

Leave this life
Having lived exquisite joy
Because of lives you influenced

The more we remember others
The more we forget ourselves

A sign of greatness is
When you can put yourself on hold
While another walks on ahead

A good deed is preceded
By a good feeling

To go the farthest
Go to the heart, then
Go to the head

An ounce of laughter
Weighs more than
A pound of trouble

Some people who talk too much
Have little to say

The more you listen
The more you realize
How little you know
The more you listen
The more you learn

Live each day with a purpose
Lay footprints worthy of following
Busy yourself looking where you are going
Glimpse back to see where you came from

Be good at something
That does good
For someone
There is no stranger in my world
Everyone is my neighbor

What you are feeling inside
Shows outside

Determine where you will find joy
Go find your joy
When you find it
Keep it
And let no one steal it

There are many things that make life rich
Cars, money, toys, entertainment, etc.
But a high richness comes
When we reconnect with a friend or friends
To talk about the good old days
So keep your friends, treat them good
One day you may find them very valuable

Just a moment
Could change a lifetime
Value each moment
For what it can do for you
Or someone else

Ask me how I am doing
Mean it
Wait for an answer
Ask more questions
Listen
Allow me to talk
Then be ready for your turn
To tell your story
I will want to hear it
Being busy helping someone
Is better than being too busy
That we walk away

I do not always have good days
Some days are bad days
But when I have a bad day
I blend it with a good attitude
And make a smoothie
And this gives me energy

To live is to learn
Stop learning
And you start dying

I don't want to feel better
Because I was right
I want to feel better
Because I had contributed
To someone feeling better

Yesterday is already a dream
And tomorrow is only a vision
But today well lived,
Makes every yesterday
A dream or happiness
And every tomorrow
A vision of hope
And while dreams and visions
Are a part of today
Allow them to color your day
And where possible
Live in them
Smile at your dream
Plan for your vision
Enjoy your today
And plant them
Water them
With sugar

And love

Sometimes the reason someone may not like you
Is because you love yourself too much

I am growing
When I am big enough
Not be annoyed by the small things

Feed a person with appreciation
He will come back to see you
And might even share with others

When we empty ourselves
We are filling someone else
When we fill ourselves
We are emptying another person
When we empty ourselves
And fill others
We are filling others and ourselves

America is great
When its goals are designed
Its people are united
Freedom is for everyone
Opportunities are welcomed
Love is its language
And its God is supreme
What part can I play
In this great America?

I am just reminding us of this one thing
Be nice, be nice, be nice
It does not cost
It pays

Thanks for walking this path with me. Hopefully, even though we might be at different intersections and you may even have stopped at a rest stop, eventually we will meet up. Happy rest of the journey and God bless you.

REFLECTIONS

Write a note to yourself about an inspiration you received while reading this book.

Write a note to yourself about what you would like to do for someone.

Write a note to yourself about a nice memorable deed someone did for you or for anyone.

Has your journey with this book helped you to be a better, more relative, more caring, and nicer person?

If you had the opportunity to meet with me, Ewart, what would you like to ask me or tell me about your experience with this book?

Reviews

A sweet daily reminder of how to live out your life's purpose. Uplifting and encouraging. A powerful reminder of how to change the world one interaction at a time.
—Cindy Quintanilla, chief encouraging officer, health management, a friend

Ewart's book reminds us to be present with those we interact with. The gift of listening we give to others surely enriches their lives.
—Lorie Long, business owner

In reading these pages, I realized that whatever your situation may be, if you apply these "words" or principals into your life, like a ointment, you will feel a great relief in your heart.
—Elias Villegas, dean of Chemeketa Community College, Woodburn Center.

The journey of reading this book will make you experience a feeling like never before. Truly powerful and life changing.
—Ari Archibald, college student

Ewart F. Brown has captured, through his life experiences, the bottom line of connecting with others for the purpose of joy. It was a thought provoking journey.
—Gary Parks, pastor relational ministries director of Oregon Conference of Seventh-day Adventists

My friend Ewart F. Brown is a godly man with a wonderfully upbeat attitude on life, who genuinely loves people. "A Candy a Day" is a wonderful life-lifting resource. The wisdom reflected here moved me to think deeper, chuckle some, occasionally shed a tear, but most importantly, determine to spend my life grasping every moment possible to build deeper relationships and touch lives in meaningful ways.
—Gary Moyer, Pastor, VP for administration, Carolina Conference of SDA, motivational speaker/trainer, life coach

About the Author

A Jamaican-born and now a citizen of the United States after living in Canada for several years. Obtained his education in Jamaica, Canada, and the United States. Since the age of twelve, Ewart began focusing toward becoming a minister, a goal he finally reached after working in sales for several companies and in nursing.

A significant work experience was working in hospitals as a psychiatric therapist and relief chaplain, where working with and understanding people took on a different and elevated meaning for him.

Pastoral ministry was his love, which gave him the opportunity to be involved in the lives of thousands of people and journeyed with them to find fulfilment in life and a hope for the future.

Ewart has retired from active church ministry and founded and is the director of Quiet Place Ministries, which allows him to travel widely as a motivational speaker, presenting seminars on Building Positive Relationships, which is helping people to get along, at home, at work, at church, and in the community.

When he is not travelling doing seminars, he spends time with family, friends, gardening, singing in nursing facilities, writing, and being involved in his community. Recently he was recognized by his city for his involvement in the community.

Ewart has a passion for people. He encourages people to value others, care for them, and change their world. He cares that people are respected and treated nicely. He says to us, be nice to one another.

CPSIA information can be obtained
at www.ICGtesting.com
Printed in the USA
BVHW06s0044300618
520402BV00006B/12/P